Interpersonal Boundaries

Interpersonal Boundaries

Variations and Violations

Edited by Salman Akhtar

JASON ARONSON
Lanham • Boulder • New York • Toronto • Oxford

Published in the United States of America
by Jason Aronson
An imprint of Rowman & Littlefield Publishers, Inc.

A wholly owned subsidiary of
The Rowman & Littlefield Publishing Group, Inc.
4501 Forbes Boulevard, Suite 200, Lanham, Maryland 20706
www.rowmanlittlefield.com

PO Box 317
Oxford
OX2 9RU, UK

British Library Cataloguing in Publication Information Available

Library of Congress Cataloging-in-Publication Data

Interpersonal boundaries: variations and violations / edited by Salman Akhtar.
   p. ; cm.
  Includes bibliographical references and index.
  ISBN-10: 0-7657-0402-1 (pbk. : alk. paper)
  ISBN-13: 978-0-7657-0402-3
  1. Self. 2. Identity (Psychology) 3. Boundaries—Psychological aspects. 4.
Personal space—Psychological aspects. 5. Interpersonal relations. 6. Child
psychology. I. Akhtar, Salman, 1946 July 31–
  [DNLM: 1. Child Development. 2. Interpersonal Relations—Child. 3. Child
Psychology. 4. Psychoanalysis. 5. Self Concept—Child.
WS 105.5.I5 I61 2006]
BF697.I678 2006
155.4'18—dc22
                                                   2005031517

Printed in the United States of America

∞™ The paper used in this publication meets the minimum requirements of
American National Standard for Information Sciences—Permanence of Paper
for Printed Library Materials, ANSI/NISO Z39.48-1992.

To the memory of
Margaret S. Mahler—
Teacher, friend, source of inspiration

Contents

Acknowledgments

The chapters in this book were originally presented at the 36th Annual Margaret S. Mahler Symposium on Child Development held on May 7, 2005, in Philadelphia. First and foremost, therefore, we wish to express our gratitude to the Margaret S. Mahler Psychiatric Research Foundation. We are also grateful to Michael Vergare, M.D., chairman, Department of Psychiatry and Human Behavior, Jefferson Medical College, as well as to the Psychoanalytic Center of Philadelphia for their shared sponsorship of the symposium. Many colleagues from the Psychoanalytic Center of Philadelphia helped during the symposium, and we remain grateful to them. Finally, we wish to acknowledge our sincere appreciation to Melissa Nevin for her efficient organization and assistance during the symposium and for her outstanding skills in the preparation of this book's manuscript.

1

The Self and Its Boundaries: An Introductory Overview

Jennifer Bonovitz, Ph.D.

To consider the matter of boundaries of various aspects of the self in health and in illness, we must first have in mind some notions about the self and how it comes to be. The very word *self* immediately brings to mind a series of questions. When does the self begin and how does it develop? What are its boundaries; what purposes do they serve? And how do they form? When does the self die or does it continue in some form after physical death? On the one hand there is a firmly bounded, somewhat illusory sense of an unchanging self that allows us to go about our lives with some assurance of continuity with our past, present, and future. On the other hand there is a more fluid, often elusive self that has many facets. Some are known to us, others are never brought to conscious awareness, but nevertheless drive our bodily sensations, emotions, thoughts, perceptions, behaviors, and relationships. This kaleidoscopic self, with its ever shifting patterns and lines of demarcation, is derived from intricate and interconnected systems of bodily and mental representations which emerge from our genetic endowment, early attachments, (Bowlby, 1969; Ainsworth et al., 1978; Main and Solomon, 1986; Fonagy, 1992), relationships with other selves, and with inanimate objects (Akhtar, 2003), as well as from cultural heritage, and ongoing encounters with everyday life. It is a self with multiple boundaries, some relatively fixed, others permeable and largely context dependent. As with the kaleidoscope, this self changes according to the angle from which it is viewed. It is subject to the vagaries of perception, memory, and affective residues of dimly remembered, forgotten, or "unthought known" experiences (Bollas, 1979).

Virginia Woolf (1928) captures the multiplicity, complexity, and contextual nature of the self and hence the impossibility of my assignment in this chapter. "[T]hese selves of which we are built up, one on top of another, as plates are piled on a waiter's hand, have attachments elsewhere, sympathies, little constitutions and rights of their own, call them what you will (and for many of these things there is no name) so that one will only come if it is raining, another in a room with green curtains, another when Mrs. Jones is not there, another if you can promise it a glass of wine—and so on; for everyone can multiply from his own experience the different terms which his different selves have made with him—and some are too wildly ridiculous to be named in print at all" (p. 251).

With this disclaimer, I will move on to identify some of the enigmas of biological, psychological, and cultural aspects of the self, and the concept of boundaries. Because of the singular importance of affect regulation in the healthy growth of psychic structures and their boundaries, I will pay particular attention to the role of fear which has proved to be a potent dysregulator of emotional well-being (LeDoux, 1996).

ENIGMAS OF THE SELF AND ITS BOUNDARIES

Across the life span there are moments of sublime intimacy, suffocating closeness, comfortable solitude, intolerable distance, and soul-destroying loneliness. The quest for optimal distance/closeness challenges us from the cradle to the grave.

Throughout life there are boundaries that protect and facilitate growth of a vibrantly alive self. Then there are boundaries or invisible roadblocks that try to protect, but end up shutting out life-giving, affective experiences so that what is left within is a starved, deadened, and empty space encased in a brittle shell. In this instance the false self has become all there is (Winnicott, 1965). The realization of this tragedy is captured in lines written by Liza, a young adult in search of a self that had been lost in childhood as she fearfully conformed to needs and wishes of her family in an attempt to ward off her terror of abandonment. "The good stuff inside me is gone, all drained out, or used up, or squashed. I am like a special dessert where all the good stuff has been spooned out and eaten. What's left is like a shell, the crust of the bread, the rind of the fruit."

The word *boundary* derives from the Latin *bodina* meaning the external or limiting line of an object, space, or area, or, something that limits or restrains. Boundaries may perform protective, life-preserving functions beginning, for example, with the skin, a biological/psychological entity whose integrity is vital to life. The skin's outer layer (*epidermis*) is without nerves and blood vessels and is nonsensitive. The inner layer (*dermis*) is highly vascular and sensitive. The boundary of the skin is of necessity both impermeable and permeable, protecting from toxins and infection, ignoring or excluding benign/unimportant levels of excitation, yet letting in nutrients (vitamin D), or medications, and processing levels of stimulation which may signal pain or exquisite pleasure. In health the "false," or social self, may be conceptualized as a protective skin or covering for the inner layer of the vulnerable "true" self. Winnicott notes that each of us has a polite or socialized self, and also a personal, private self that is not available except in intimacy. "If you look around you see that *in health* this splitting of the self is an achievement of personal growth; *in illness* the split is a matter of a schism in the mind that can go to any depth, at its deepest it is labeled schizophrenia" (quoted in Abram, 1997, p. 281).

THE BEGINNINGS OF THE SELF

There is no agreement when the self begins—that question has been a matter of philosophical, theological, ethical, and biological debate. Does it begin with conception when the sperm bursts through the boundary of the egg, thus forming a new entity now bounded not only by the mother's womb, but by her fantasies about the new life she carries within? (Stern, 1995) We know that even in utero the fetus is sensitive to the mother's voice, to the rhythms of her body. The mother simultaneously enters into imaginative dialogue with the infant who is so much a part of her, yet hidden from her view and touch. The ghosts, both good and bad, in the mother's nursery hover around as she slips into her new identity (Fraiberg, 1987). Then comes entry into the world outside of the mother's protective body. Now the infant is on her own, in terms of drawing breath and actively seeking not only food, but emotional nutrients to sustain life. The cutting of the cord is the first of many separations on the road to becoming an individuated yet attached entity in the external world of other selves and the internal world of self and object representations.

I now return to consideration of the infant's skin which provides the protective envelope surrounding the as yet undeveloped and unintegrated bits and pieces of the physical and psychological selves. The skin replaces the mother's womb as the demarcation of inner from outer. How the mother appreciates its sensitivity, handles and protects the skin in the course of bathing, changing, feeding, and cuddling, is of utmost importance for how this vital organ will be treated, as the child assumes responsibility for its care and for its use in calling up images of the mother. In her seminal paper on the role of the skin in early object relations, Bick (1968) writes of the infant's subjective experience as follows. "The thesis is that in its most primitive form the parts of the personality are felt to have no binding force amongst themselves and must therefore be held together passively, by the skin functioning as a boundary" (p. 484). She emphasizes that the internal function of containing parts of the self is dependent on the possibility of introjecting an external object capable of performing this function. "Until the containing functions have been introjected, the concept of a space within the self cannot arise" (p. 484).

TWO CASE VIGNETTES

The Case of Colin

Colin's mother clearly adored him as an infant and toddler. In one of many affectionate gestures she gently caressed the soft skin on his face and neck with her silken cheek. On his first day of preschool at age two years, Colin, in a low-keyed moment, was observed to use the silk binding of his blanket to rub gently against his face and neck. It seemed that the toddler was using the gestures of his absent mother to comfort himself and after a few minutes of this, combined with the encouragement of a sensitive teacher, he was able to return to play with the other children.

The Case of Annie

Annie's mother scrubbed her face and hands to the point of redness and wiped her nose vigorously, oblivious to the child's protesting screams (behaviors described by child's father). During the early sessions of therapy with me, four-year-old Annie comforted herself after mother left the room (she often left to obtain relief in solitude) by taking a nail file she found in my desk drawer and rubbing it up and down her arm. She became distraught when I tried to substitute a gentler comforter. At bedtime she picked at the skin on her arms and legs until they bled. Each child used an object at hand to stimulate the skin surface and thus to recreate a familiar feeling of connection following separation from the mother.

The infant's need for physical and emotional proximity to the caregiver, for gentle touch, loving gaze, and competent holding, is a matter of survival. Bowlby's pioneer work on the attachment system and the profound effects of early loss on the child's physical and emotional integrity has been elaborated and substantiated by researchers in the fields of psychoanalysis; infant research; neurobiology; and psychiatry. Spitz has given us heartrending film footage of the painful, sometimes fatal consequences of emotional deprivation for infants raised in the vacuum of physical provision devoid of emotional investment. "There is in infants an inbuilt need to be in touch with and to cling to a human being. In this sense there is a need for an object which is independent of food, a need which is as primary as the need for food and warmth" (Bowlby, 1958). The mother's (and others') enfolding arms protect the baby from "falling forever," from the fear of annihilation (Winnicott, 1989), from physical harm, and most important from fear.

FEAR: INNATE PROTECTOR AND POTENTIAL DESTROYER OF THE SECURELY BOUNDED SELF

Neuroscientist Joseph LeDoux (1996) has compellingly documented that fear is a primordial emotion designed to signal danger. In infancy and early childhood prolonged separation from, or frightening behavior of, attachment figures triggers the fear system which is mediated by the amygdala. This tiny but powerful command center alerts the sympathetic, parasympathetic, and hypothalamic-pituitary-adrenal systems. Results include increase in heart rate and blood pressure, increase in blood flow and glucose to the skeletal muscles, shutdown of nonessential functions, and release of a cascade of neurotransmitter responses. These mechanisms normally shut down when the danger passes. However, children subjected to repeated separations, abuse, or neglect at the hands of needed attachment figures remain in a state of painful hyperarousal of the fear system which in LeDoux's words "hijacks the rest of the brain." An emotion designed to alert and protect transforms into one that invades and damages not only psychic structures, but physical structures of the brain (Heim, Meinlschmidt, and Nemeroff, 2003).

Fear-inducing assaults on the child's physical and/or, emotional self lacerate the cocoon of safety essential for the development of affect regulation and of positive internal representations of self and other, and of self-with-other. Indelible memories come unbidden to haunt the future. The usual, ordinary, expectancy of safety in the interpersonal world is no longer available to bind anxiety, contain persecutory images, and soothe painful sensations. Psychological functions vital for emotional well-being, such as empathy, reality testing, or the capacity for reflective functioning, are compromised (Fonagy, 1992, 2001). Subjectively these children feel abandoned by loving, good, internal objects which provide and contain. Instead they feel at the mercy of attacks by hateful and hating objects. They are more sensitized to and likely to experience affects in the negative or defensive spectrum including anger, shame, disgust, distaste and their derivative feelings of embarrassment, humiliation, envy, and contempt. They have a greater vulnerability to painful/terrifying ruptures in the integrity of the self under stress and are prone to violate the psychological boundaries of others in attempts to restabilize, or, to attract others who will be unconsciously drawn to violate them.

TWO MORE CASE VIGNETTES

The Case of Julie

Julie was brought for treatment at age eight years because of her oppositional tendencies, her aversion to being touched or held, and her aggressive behavior toward her three younger siblings whom she terrorized by pushing them against hard surfaces and yelling that she was going to kill them. Her behavior was puzzling given the empathy and emotional availability of her parents and grandparents. A careful history shed light on the situation. Julie had been restrained by her mother every six months from age nine months to age five years for diagnostic X-ray procedures. These had been terrifying experiences, all the more so because, in the child's eyes, her mother had participated as an aggressor. Julie was afraid of her mother's touch, even proximity, and used anger to keep her at what felt like a "safe" distance. As soon as she could muster the strength, the child became the aggressor, pushing her siblings against hard surfaces just as she had been pushed onto a hard surface for the X-rays.

Rage in the infant is a biologically driven response to excessive fear or pain and while often secondary to environmental factors, its intensity may also depend upon inborn, unusual sensory sensitivities, or upon temperament. The rage response is a communication to caregivers that help is needed urgently to restore a sense of safety and relief from painful stimuli. When help comes quickly, the infant or young child's construct of a secure boundary that protects the integrity of the developing self is strengthened. Over time this is internalized and may be visualized as a protective internal holding of the self which provides a barrier against impingements from internal or external sources of disturbance.

Conversely, persistent states of anger rob the child of the capacity to evoke security-inducing images of, and a sense of connection to, loving attachment figures. The protective holding and sustaining function of the self is feeble or entirely absent. The use of fear as a signal function to accurately perceive danger, and to reflect upon a protective response, is frequently lost, perhaps never developed. The important capacity to use affect as a signal is not present at birth. Rather, it is a developmental achievement arising out of ongoing mutual exchanges with an emotionally sensitive caregiver who can mirror, contain, and give words to what the infant might be feeling. Children deprived of empathic parents who contain and metabolize painful feelings grow up avoidant of the contents of their inner lives. This is eloquently expressed by a patient whose mother, though well intentioned, was "mindless" when it came to the feelings of her children. Father was prone to outbursts of rage. "Please do not ask me about my 'inner life.' I do not want to go there and neither do you, I'm not sure what it looks like but I know it hurts to see it. I don't know what it is but I know when you see it and feel it. It makes you want to die right on the spot."

Eagle (2003) notes that a sense of security "facilitates exploration and serves to regulate negative affect" (p. 29). Sandler (2003) suggests that fear and the need for safety prompt the child's developing ego to engage not only in defensive activity, but to heighten the feeling of safety by the means of modification and control of perception. He posits that the child's fearful re-action to separation and the ways in which he/she tries to regain a feeling of safety becomes internalized in an internal object relationship which affects the ways the individual will later interact with others. "Each partner, at any given moment, has a role for the other, and unconsciously negotiates with the other to get him or her to respond in a particular way; and these roles are intimately bound up with what can be conceptualized as internal object re-lations" (p. 15). Sandler's hypothesis is supported by research on how the brain constructs perceptions. Contrary to the intuitive idea that our brains simply take in the world as it really is, every perception is the end result of a process of matching current external stimuli with patterns that are already encoded in the brain. Since the brain strives for only "good enough" matches, current perceptions are strongly biased by previous perceptions. This has special relevance for transference and countertransference phe-nomena both in and outside of treatment (Pally, 1997).

Children who consistently, over time, experienced abuse or neglect seem to maintain a core self and inner working model of self-with-other that is suf-fused with negative growth-stunting emotions (Emde, 1999). The internal sense of self is easily threatened, while the internal sense of other is en-crusted with fearful suspicion and has to be kept at a distance from the vul-nerable self. Such a configuration is resistant to change and frequently robs the child of potential sources of emotional nourishment in the here and now. The individual maintains a strong tie to the "bad," inconstant object. It is as though an impenetrable wall has been constructed around the internalized tie to the bad object.

The Case of Michael

Michael, a 10-year-old boy, had been shuffled back and forth between dysfunctional, neglectful family members as an infant and toddler. He came to rest with an aunt who was alternately overwhelmed and depressed, or frenetically active in her attempts to ward off depression. Her anger found outlet in beatings and angry tirades. When he was five, a friendly neighbor took Michael under her wing on a daily basis. She included him in her family's meals and outings, helped with his school projects and took him on vacations. Yet Michael continued to feel, and behave, as though he had no expectation of anything good in his present life, or, despite his many talents, worth striving for in the future. He stole from the neighbor and destroyed her property, eventually provoking her to abandon him after he spat in her daughter's soda during a birthday party being given for him.

One could conceptualize Michael's predicament as one of boundary formation gone awry. The intrapsychic formation bounded so firmly within him was painful yet enduring, and presumably reassuring. He knew its contours, could rely on its predictable characteristics, and implicitly knew how to get others to cooperate in fortifying it even further. In a peculiar way he felt at home with it. In Mahler's view (Mahler, Pine, and Bergman, 1975) attainment of positively balenced object constancy depends upon internalization of a positive image of the mothering figure and in particular on fusion of the "good" and the "bad" object into a unified whole. This unification had not taken place in Michael, leaving him vulnerable to fits of rage and hatred against both himself and others.

CULTURAL BOUNDARIES OF THE SELF

Culture here is used in a broad sense to include ethnicity and socioeconomic factors. It consists of shared language, customs, religious practices, inanimate objects, visual images, sounds, smells, foods, and child care practices. From the beginning infants take in aspects of their cultural surrounds including the tones and rhythms of language, distinctive smell, sound and color of mother and father, of food eaten, tactile sensation and visual images of clothing, music played in the home, and so on. Day-to-day cultural experiences in the external world eventually become enduring representations in the internal world, interwoven with the sense of self and of other. Many cultures set strong limits on which behaviors, types of touch, forms of address, modes of dress, foods, social activities, and religious practices are permitted. Some groups fiercely protect their cultural identity and discourage intermingling with other cultures by building a barricade of prohibitions designed to prevent intrusion from without. Adolescence can be particularly challenging for these insular communities as their young people's sense of belonging and loyalty to their culture of origin may come into conflict with their wish to belong to and identify with a broader, less confining culture (Levy-Warren, 1996).

Psychoanalytic theory and practice have to a large extent remained color-blind and culture bound. There have been somewhat harsh critiques of the cultural myopia of Mahler's separation-individuation theory (Kirschener,

1996). There are, however, some encouraging efforts to examine the contributions of ethnic, racial, socioeconomic, religious, and linguistic differences to the formation of the sense of self, its boundaries, and its internal structures, as well as the implications for treatment (Akhtar, 1998, 1999). Skillful clinical work with patients requires both immersion in, and optimal distance from, the sociocultural, ethnic characteristics of all participants. "Where the therapist's cultural background is very similar to that of the patient, problems will arise with optimal distance. Where there is great diversity, the problem will be around empathic immersion" (Bonovitz, 1998, p. 174).

In one of the few in-depth explorations reported in the psychoanalytic literature, Mehta (1998) describes the emergence of conflicts in cultural identity and the ego ideal, use of defensive splitting, sexual fantasies linked to culture, and heightened ambivalence in the mother-daughter relationship arising from cultural disparities between the generations. Freeman's (1998) study of Japanese child rearing thoughtfully elaborates the relationship between culture and child development, addressing both cultural and intrapsychic dimensions. The inner world of personal thoughts and true feelings is tightly bound and hidden from others (one's backside). The "front side" which is shown to others, is characterized by "refined cooperative restraint, reserve and deference" (p. 20). He explains how cultural sensitivity to shame, and reticence in expression of private thoughts and feelings verbally to another, deter Japanese patients from seeking therapy.

Since much of the culturally derived self resides in implicit knowing, we are all vulnerable to a state of "mindlessness" when it comes to observation and empathic understanding of difference. More malignantly we may respond from a rigid defensiveness by viewing cultural differences with antipathy or contempt, even hatred. For the purposes of this chapter I will very briefly address only two dimensions of culturally influenced differences. These relate to time and optimal distance.

Time

I include these comments on the dimension of time because I believe it is a hidden regulator of intimacy. In Western nations there is a notable tendency to use time to distance, even to justify avoidance of direct personal contact. When the Western concept of time is forced upon immigrant families who are accustomed to different rhythms of life, a feeling of disorientation results. In an attempt to restabilize, they may make attempts to slow things down, to hold on to the other, in a way that is mistakenly experienced as boundary crossing.

Speaking of Western, industrialized countries, Akhtar (1999) notes that time gradually became tied to the accumulation of capital. As a result efficiency and punctuality have become highly valued contributors to the "bottom line."

This has led to a concept of time that resides in the *mind* and bears a dollar sign. Akhtar contrasts this to nonindustrialized nations "where the manufacture of commodities did not take over the community, the beginning and ending of various social get-togethers continued to depend upon the arrival of loved ones (often by treacherously unreliable means) and the permissive winks of gods and seasons" (p. 117). The sense of time operative here is poetically called the "time of the heart or the time of love" (p. 117). I was deeply impressed by culturally defined differences in the concept of time during a recent visit to a small rural village in Nicaragua. Unlike my host family, I was eager, even fretful to know the time of our departure so I could be ready. Their responses to my polite inquiries were vague, noncommittal. It didn't really matter when we left, there were no clocks at the other end to mark the time of our arrival or departure. The last mile or so of the journey was made on foot; there was no road. Nobody in the village had felt a great need to take the time to build one. When we arrived, everyone stopped what they were doing, if indeed they were doing anything, to gather around us. There was no pressure of time; activity was governed more by the heat and the need to avoid overheating by excessive movement. Occasionally someone moved to tend to a child, or to draw water from a nearby well for cooling and drinking purposes, otherwise we sat quietly, talking from time to time.

All this is in stark contrast to life in urban communities of the United States where watches and clocks, schedules and deadlines are prominent organizers of every minute. I thought of children dropped off in the waiting room of my office, with their electronic games or cell phones, their parents rushing off to do errands, while adult patients arrive with their cell phones and laptops so that no minute is "wasted" just sitting with the self. Preoccupation with electronic devices which constantly either connect us with others (the cell phone) or stimulate the brain from without with rapidly moving images and changing sounds may perhaps be an attempt to avoid an internal loneliness indicative of an impact of technology on separation-individuation processes. At least in many urban/suburban communities of the United States, there seems to be a diminishing desire, perhaps capacity, to be alone (Winnicott, 1958).

Optimal Distance

The cultural nuances of optimal distance are especially relevant when treating immigrant families to avoid pathologizing separation-individuation processes that are different rather than deviant. Cultural sensitivity is required to understand why, for example, Indian parents brought their adolescent daughter for treatment with the pained complaint that she wants to be "too American, she doesn't listen to us anymore." In fact these parents would not have sought me out at all had they not known that I am myself an immigrant and aware of cross-cultural issues.

Akhtar (1992) offers the definition that "optimal distance is best viewed as a psychic position that permits intimacy without loss of autonomy" (p. 30). Cross-cultural studies of the family and of child-rearing patterns provide data that there are indeed significant differences in the value given to intimacy versus autonomy. Roland's (1989, 1996) work with Japanese and Indian families, both in their homelands and in New York, led him to conclude that Mahler's separation-individuation theory, with its emphasis on autonomy, initiative, and self-reliance cannot be applied to understanding the psyche of either group. Observations of Indian families led him to coin the term *symbiosis-reciprocity* to describe how the inner world is organized around images of "we," "our," and "us," rather than "I" or "me." Much more so than in primarily industrialized countries, there are hierarchical relationships within the family defined by kinship positions, birth order, and gender. Ego boundaries are more permeable within the family. These are characteristics I have observed in treating South American families who grew up in rural areas.

Mahler et al. (1975) write, "Consciousness of self and absorption without awareness of the self are two polarities between which (the normal adult) moves within varying ease and with varying degrees of alternation or simultaneity" (p. 3). It would appear that in Western culture the separation-individuation process leads to greater consciousness of the autonomous self. Children are raised to leave home. In Asian cultures the emphasis is more toward the polarity of absorption within the greater unity of the family with less consciousness of an individuated self. Children are raised to stay within the bounds of the extended kinship unit. In Roland's (1989) words, "The normal separation, privacy, and autonomy of Western style relationships and the psychological space around oneself disappear into the more symbiotic mode of giving and asking, of caring for and depending on, of influencing and being influenced" (p. 226).

Kakar (1985) emphasizes the innate capacity of the baby to adapt to the cultural environment in which it was born. He notes that it is common, for example, to have patients who slept in their mother's bed until puberty. What might be considered sexual overstimulation and disruptive to boundary formation for a child in a Western middle-class family may be simply a matter of adaptation to the average expectable environment in another culture.

CONCLUSION

In this introductory chapter I have laid the foundation for consideration of the complexities of the self and its boundaries. I identified some of the enigmatic questions pertaining to biological, psychological, and cultural aspects of the self and the many boundary issues which ensue. In the chapters which follow the authors give us a more microscopic view, each from the perspective of a wealth of clinical data skillfully integrated with theory. Dr. Tyson takes a developmental, integrative approach to boundary formation in children, drawing primarily on the theoretical frameworks of Bowlby, Mahler, and Winnicott. Her chapter is elaborated upon by Dr. Garfield. Dr. Gabbard takes us to the dark side with his discussion of boundary-violating therapists and their patients. His chapter is discussed by Dr. Brenner, who offers us some very interesting clinical material of his own. Finally, Dr. Kogan presents extraordinary clinical material detailing the harrowing analytic work with a severely traumatized man. This account of a very difficult analysis is elucidated and contained by the incisive discussion of Dr. Akhtar. It is my hope that the three main contributions to this book (namely those of Tyson, Gabbard, and Kogan) and their respective discussions (by Garfield, Brenner, and Akhtar) as well as the concluding commentary on all this material by Dr. Henri Parens will add significantly to our knowledge of boundaries of the self. This knowledge should, in turn, enhance our therapeutic skills in dealing with some of our most difficult patients.

REFERENCES

Abram, J. (1997). *The Language of Winnicott: A Dictionary and Guide to Understanding His Work.* Northvale, NJ: Jason Aronson.

Ainsworth, M. D. S., et al. (1978). *Patterns of Attachment: A Psychological Study of the Strange Situation.* Hillsdale, NJ: Lawrence Erlbaum.

Akhtar, S. (1992). Tethers, orbits, and invisible fences: Clinical, developmental, sociocultural, and technical aspects of optimal distance. In *When the Body Speaks: Psychological Meanings in Kinetic Cues*, ed. S. Kramer and S. Akhtar, pp. 21–57. Northvale, NJ: Jason Aronson.

———. (1998). Psychoanalysis and the rainbow of cultural authenticity. In: *Colors of Childhood: Separation-Individuation across Cultural, Racial, and Ethnic Differences*, ed. S. Kramer and S. Akhtar, pp. 113–128. Northvale, NJ: Jason Aronson.

———. (1999). *Immigration and Identity: Turmoil, Treatment, and Transformation.* Northvale, NJ: Jason Aronson.

———. (2003). Things: Developmental, clinical, and technical aspects of inanimate objects. *Canadian Journal of Psychoanalysis* 11:21–44.

Bick, E. (1968). The experience of the skin in early object relations. *International Journal of Psycho-Analysis* 49:484–486.

Bollas, C. (1979). *Being a Character: Psychoanalysis and Self Experience.* New York: Hill and Wang.

Bonovitz, J. (1998). Reflections of the self in the cultural looking glass. In: *The Colors of Childhood: Separation-Individuation across Cultural, Racial and Ethnic Differences*, ed. S. Kramer and S. Akhtar, pp. 169–198. Northvale, NJ: Jason Aronson.

Bowlby, J. (1951). Maternal Care and Maternal Health. *Bulletin of the World Health Organization* 3:355–534.

———. (1958). The nature of the child's tie to his mother. *International Journal of Psychoanalysis* 39:350–73.

———. (1969). *Attachment and Loss, Vol. 1*. London: Hogarth Press.

Eagle, M. (2003). Clinical implications of attachment. *Psychoanalytic Inquiry* 23:27–53.

Emde, R. (1999). Moving ahead: Integrating influences of affective processes for development and for psychoanalysis. *International Journal of Psycho-Analysis* 80:317–339.

Fonagy, P. (1992). A theory of the child's theory of mind. *Cognition* 44:283–296.

———. (1999). The transgenerational transmission of holocaust trauma: Lessons learned from the analysis of an adolescent with obsessive compulsive disorder. *Attachment and Human Development* 1:92–114.

———. (2001). *Attachment Theory and Psychoanalysis*. New York: Guilford Press.

Fraiberg, S. (1987). Ghosts in the nursery: A psychoanalytic approach to the problems of impaired mother-infant relationships. In *Selected Writings of Selma Fraiberg*, pp. 100–136. Columbus: Ohio State University Press.

Freeman, D. (1998). Emotional refueling in development, mythology and cosmology: The Japanese separation-individuation experience. In *Colors of Childhood: Separation-Individuation across Cultural, Racial, and Ethnic Differences*, eds. S. Akhtar and S. Kramer, pp. 17–60. Northvale, NJ: Jason Aronson.

Heim, C., Meinlschmidt, M., and Nemeroff, C. (2003). Neurobiology of early-life stress. *Psychiatric Annals* 23:18–26

Kakar, S. (1985). Psychoanalysis and non-western cultures. *International Review of Psychoanalysis* 12:441–448.

Kirschener, S. (1996). *The Religious and Romantic Origins of Psychoanalysis: Individuation and Integration into Post-Freudian Theory*. New York: Cambridge University Press.

LeDoux, J. (1996). *The Emotional Brain: The Mysterious Underpinnings of Emotional Life*. New York: Touchstone.

Levy-Warren, M. (1996). *The Adolescent Journey: Development, Identity Formation, and Psychotherapy*. Northvale, NJ: Jason Aronson.

Mahler, M. S., and Fuher, M. (1968). *On Human Symbiosis and the Vicissitudes of Individuation*. New York: International Universities Press.

Mahler, M. S., Pine, F., and Bergman, A. (1975). *The Psychological Birth of the Human Infant: Symbiosis and Individuation*. New York: Basic.

Main, M., and Solomon, J. (1986). Discovery of an insecure-disorganized/disoriented attachment pattern. In *Affective Development in Infancy*, eds. T. B. Brazelton and M. W. Yogman, pp. 95–124. Norwood, NJ: Ablex.

Mehta, P. (1998). The emergence, conflicts, and integration of the bicultural self: Psychoanalysis of an adolescent daughter of South-Asian immigrant parents. In *Colors of Childhood: Separation-Individuation across Cultural, Racial, and Ethnic Differences*, eds. S. Kramer and S. Akhtar, pp. 129–168. Northvale, NJ: Jason Aronson.

Pally, R. (1997). Developments in neuroscience 11: How the brain actively constructs perceptions. *International Journal of Psychoanalysis* 78:1021–1030.

Roland, A. (1989). *In Search of Self in India and Japan*. Princeton, NJ: Princeton University Press.

———. (1996). *Cultural Pluralism and Psychoanalysis: The Asian and North American Experience*. New York: Rutledge.

Sandler, J. (2003). On attachment to internal objects. *Psychoanalytic Inquiry* 23:12–26.

Stern, D. (1995). *The Motherhood Constellation: A Unified View of Parent-Child Psychotherapy*. London: Karnac Books.

Winnicott, D. W. (1958). The capacity to be alone. *International Journal of Psycho-Analysis* 39:416–26.

———. (1965). *The Maturational Processes and the Facilitating Environment: Studies in the Theory of Emotional Development*. New York: International Universities Press.

———. (1989). *Psycho-Analytic Explorations*. C. Winnicott, R. Shepherd, and M. Davis, eds. London: Karnac Books.

Woolf, V. (1928). *Orlando*, quoted from the 1994 large print edition Oxford: Isis Publishing Press, p. 251.

2

Boundary Formation in Children: Normality and Pathology

Phyllis Tyson, Ph.D.

What we call boundary violations are of increasing concern in our profession, in our society, in our churches, and in our homes, as reports surface about physical and sexual transgressions between parent and child, priest and altar boy, therapist and patient. Seemingly the definition of what constitutes a boundary violation appears to differ from one person to the next, one facet of society to another. What is considered a boundary violation by some might be considered average expectable behavior or even entitlement by another. To make optimal adaptation to the boundaries society has established requires a sense of inner psychological boundaries: between self and other, between parts of the self. As far as we can tell, the very young infant has little or no conceptual sense of psychological separateness from the mother. Our task today is to try to understand how, from this state of mother-infant oneness, the child forms and develops the capacity to maintain objective and clear self and object psychological boundaries, and also to understand what goes wrong when a child or adult fails to form or to maintain self and object boundaries.

Psychological interest in the mind of the child, beginning from earliest infancy, dates back at least as far as Freud's hypothesis that at birth the infant was in a state of primary narcissism. When Benedek described parenthood as a developmental phase, she thought the mother and child functioned as a biological symbiotic unit. Many have studied the mother-infant unity. Perhaps most notable among these, with the longest lasting legacy, are Bowlby, Mahler, and Winnicott. Each has assumed a different vantage point and there has been considerable debate about the merits and shortcomings of one approach versus the other. However, for our task today of understanding boundary formation, I suggest that instead of the either/or debate we gain more by converging their theories. In so doing we can define three fundamental modes of experiencing that emerge from the primary unity of mother and infant: experiencing within the relationship, experiencing the emerging self, and experiencing the potential space between the two. Although the nature of the experience in each mode is different, all are interdependent, and each provides the context for the others.

There are many challenges along the developmental pathways as children and their parents experience themselves and each other in these various modes. Ideally what emerges in the course of these various modes of experiencing is the formation and capacity to maintain objective and clear self and object psychological boundaries. The first steps are taken in early childhood; adolescence offers another opportunity. Ultimately, maintaining stable self and other psychological boundaries becomes an ongoing lifelong task that some may be unable to fully master—witness the increasing concern about boundary violations in our profession. Indeed, I think there are subtle or not so subtle ways that most of us at times unconsciously function as if we are unclear where one mind stops and another begins.

To understand this process of forming psychological boundaries between self and other, I shall begin with two very brief clinical vignettes from young children who I have recently discussed at length and one longer one from the analysis of an adolescent that demonstrate the difficulties some children have in forming and maintaining stable boundaries. I shall then elaborate on this notion of three modes of experiencing: experiencing the relationship, experiencing the emerging self, and experiencing the potential space between the two. I shall then describe how self and object psychological boundaries might emerge from these modes of experiencing. Finally I shall describe what I think are some of the important developmental processes, pathways, and stumbling blocks a child negotiates in the course of these experiences which might enhance or interfere with objective psychological boundary formation.

THREE CLINICAL VIGNETTES

I. Susie

Susie, age three and a half, was angry that her mother would not let her have ice cream before her early morning session. Her mother responded to her provocations by spanking her. Wailing, she enters my consulting room, picks up a pair of scissors, and lunges at me with fury, shouting, "Get away from me, you horrible mean monster!"

II. Colin

Colin, age four, felt angry and abandoned when I returned from a short vacation. Coming into my office on the day I returned he heard some children playing outside and he imagined that I played with those children instead of seeing him—I must like them better. He was quickly overcome with jealousy. Chewing up a plastic baby doll, he claimed that he wanted to "kill all the children in the world." He shouted profanities and murderous threats to the children outside, and as he became increasingly anxious, his feelings and his perceptions of me became increasingly blurred. He picked up a play sword and lunged at me, shouting "Monster!" "I'll kill you."

III. Danielle

Danielle began analysis at the age of 16, complaining of compulsive overeating, an inability to lose weight, and a sense of being overly dependent on her parents. Although D. saw herself to be much like her father, she felt totally preoccupied with idealization, hatred, wishes to compete with and fears of separation from her mother. She would swing from intense loving to intense hatred of her. She saw her mother as slim, smart, assertive, and successful in her career, i.e., all the things that D. wanted for herself. A session from the second year of her analysis gives a sample of her preoccupation.

She began a session saying, "I just had a surge of anxiety. I was thinking about the prom. Will anyone ask me? What will I wear? I'll never look as good as that picture of my mother taken when she was 18. There I go again, always comparing myself to my mother." She added, insightfully, "Until I start to see my mother as a real person, I won't get anywhere. Otherwise, I think if I get ahead it's like murdering mother. Aha, murder mother, marry father!" She laughed nervously. "Now I feel anxious, I can't think, I have a complete block. I feel stupid; now I feel mad at you, like it's your fault I have a mental block. Suddenly I feel an urge to see my mother."

She came in the next day declaring that she was feeling in an angry mood. Then she described a dream. "I'm with two guys, and there's a trapeze and rings. I tried to get on the trapeze. A guy lifts me up, I can't believe he can pick me up so easily. Then he got on the rings. The dream switches, and the guy on the rings is kissing a witch, a wicked lady. She throws him into a pool, he is trapped there until I grow walrus tusks on my vagina."

She thought the witch must represent her mother, or me. "But, she said, she is also a part of me, the mean self-critical voice; I can't get away from her.

Yet she was the way I'd like to be, slim and attractive, she could attract the man. In the dream I was mad at this guy, because he stopped the game with me to be with the witch. I can't even win in competition with a witch! I think I'm mad that I gave in to her and grew the tusks. But it shows how afraid I am of sex, no one could get near me if I grew tusks. A walrus is fat, it's about the way I see myself, fat and ugly." Then she said, "I just had a vision of myself completely angry, tearing my hair out, all the rage is out of control, but it's turned on me. I just had a vision of my Mom, sitting behind me, laughing at me. It's funny, one minute I think we are pals, then I hate her, then I love her, then I hate her. I feel like a dog on a chain running around in circles never close, but never far."

MODES OF EXPERIENCING

I. The Attachment System

Shortly after birth, the infant and the mother establish what Bowlby referred to as a reciprocal affective feedback loop, an attachment system, which assures the infant's survival. Within this attachment system there is ideally a mutual exchange of intimacy, dependence, care, and affection. From the safety of this system the infant forms a firm attachment to the mother. This attachment provides the matrix for all future relationships. Hypothesizing that there is biologically driven motive for attachment at least as strong as the dual drives posited by Freud, Bowlby and subsequent researchers studying attachment focus on the *system*, and the patterns or form of the attachment that emerge from this system. They use the capacity for relatedness, and a continuing maturity or immaturity in relationships, as the major way of measuring the normality or pathology of the developmental process. Guntrip (1969), for example, refers to "the emotional dynamics of the infant's growth in experiencing himself as 'becoming a person' in meaningful relationships, first with the mother, then the family, and finally with the ever enlarging world outside" (p. 243). While Guntrip does not completely neglect the development of the individual as a separate entity, his focus is on attachment and relatedness: "Meaningful relationships are those which enable the infant to find himself as a person through experiencing his own significance for other people and their significance for him, thus endowing his existence with those values of human relationship which make life purposeful and worth living" (p. 243).

II. Separation-Individuation

From within the envelope of this attachment system the infant also engages the process of what Mahler called separation-individuation. Mahler's focus was the *inner world*: ego functioning, the sense of self. She wondered how, from a mother/infant dual unity, an ego forms which functions to ensure self-regulation and to enable the child to define a sense of self as a separate individual with his own thoughts, feelings, sensations, and separate identity.

There has been considerable tension in discussions among psychoanalysts as to the utility of the term *self* or of *ego*. This tension seems to originate from the term Freud (1923) used to describe the psychic apparatus. For instead of using the ordinary term for self he used *das Ich*, which referred to both ego and self. Freud's conception of selfhood, therefore, appears to have implied a necessary tension between the person as a subject, "I"—a wishful, subjectively experienced, but also potentially rational agent—and the person as "me"—an object of self-knowledge. The "me" part of the self is the *categorical* or *representational* self, the inner organization of attitudes, beliefs, desires, and values. A sense of "me" relies on a capacity to view and reflect on the self objectively, as an object among other objects. Such self-reflection requires a capacity for what Fonagy and his colleagues (2002) refer to as *mentalization* or *reflective function*—an awareness that thoughts and feelings are lodged internally, in the mind, and a capacity to think about and reflect upon one's thoughts and feelings and to also realize that others also have thoughts and feelings, beliefs and desires. The capacity to think about one's own thoughts as well as what is in the mind of the other facilitates boundary formation.

The "I" part of the self-concept refers to the sense of oneself as an active agent. The "I" self is the intentional designer, creator, initiator, organizer, actor, regulator, and manager of all activity. The "I" self subjectively experiences thinking one's thoughts and feeling one's feelings, not simply reflexively reacting to the outside environment.

In another context I have examined the concept of agency and its developmental formation, which I shall briefly summarize. At its most basic level, agency requires (1) an awareness that the self possesses a force that can bring about action, (2) an awareness that the self is the instrument of that action, and (3) an awareness that self-actions beget change (see Fonagy et al., 2002). To these cognitive processes, Fonagy and his colleagues (2002) add a fourth: intentionality. An intentional mental being, using the capacity for *mentalization* or *reflective function*, recognizes that actions are deliberate; they are executed with the intent of making a change, reaching a particular goal. As an intentional mental being a child eventually comes to understand that not only are actions deliberate, but that there are links between actions and feelings; particular feeling states can result from specific actions; and one can have intentions or desires without acting on them.

To these four elements I have (2005) suggested a fifth: *self-responsibility*. Once the "I" self is subjectively experienced as a separate, individuated, intentional agent, the chief executive of all thoughts, feelings, desires, and actions, this "I" self becomes accountable for those thoughts, feelings, desires, and actions. Self-responsibility involves "owning up to one's needs and impulses as one's own" (Loewald, 1979, p. 392). As I shall discuss later, forming and maintaining boundaries relies on self-responsibility. Self-responsibility means admitting guilt; acknowledging ownership of one's emotions, one's angry, hateful, envious, jealous, competitive, vengeful, destructive, greedy, and murderous feelings; and not blaming others for them.

Self-responsibility also involves mastery. Angry feelings, for example, in their many forms, as well as the whole spectrum of emotions, are ubiquitous; they are part of the human condition. Conflicts, at whatever developmental level and whether they are interpersonal or intrapsychic, can never be fully "resolved" because the emotional challenges that arouse these feelings are also part of the human condition, and so inescapable. The developmental challenge therefore is not resolution, it is *mastery*—owning these feelings, desires, and impulses, gaining control over them and then finding the most adaptive way of expressing them. This means that the individual must recognize that while the words or actions of another may arouse intense feelings, the feelings aroused and the response belong to the self.

III. Potential Space

A third mode of experience, I suggest, is what Winnicott described as the potential space between the mother and infant. *Potential space* is the general term Winnicott used to refer to an intermediate area of experiencing, an experiencing that lies between fantasy and reality. Potential space can include the area of the transitional object and transitional phenomena, the area of play space, the area of analytic space, the area of cultural experience, and the area of creativity. And while this potential space might originate in a (potential) physical and mental space between mother and infant, i.e., within a dyad, during the course of normal development it becomes possible for the child (or adult) to develop his own capacity to generate potential space. The concept of potential space remains somewhat enigmatic, partly because it is couched within Winnicott's idiosyncratic language system of images and metaphors. However, I think it can be usefully viewed as another mode or way of experiencing that helps us to understand psychological boundaries and their formation. Winnicott described potential space variously as:

> "Potential space is an intermediate area of experiencing that lies between (a) the inner world, 'inner psychic reality'" . . . and (b) "actual or external reality."
> . . . It lies "between the subjective object and the object objectively perceived, between me-extensions and not-me" . . . The essential feature [of this area of experiencing in general and the transitional object in particular] is . . . the par-

adox, and the acceptance of the paradox: the baby creates the object, but the object was there waiting to be created. . . . In the rules of the game we all know that we will never challenge the baby to elicit an answer to the question: did you create that or did you find it?" (1968, p. 89); "Potential space both joins and separates the infant (child, or adult) and the mother (object). This is the paradox that I accept and do not attempt to resolve. The baby's separating-out of the world of objects from the self is achieved only through the absence of a space between [the infant and mother], the potential space being filled in the way that I am describing' (i.e., with illusion, with playing and with symbols)." (1971, p. 108)

Ogden (1985) suggests that the idea of potential space might become clearer if we see it as a dialectical process, "a process in which two opposing concepts each create, inform, preserve, and negate the other, each standing in a dynamic, ever changing relationship with the other" (p. 129). Winnicott claims that in the beginning "there is no such thing as a baby. There is also no such thing as a mother (an objectively conceptualized mother). Instead there is the illusionary mother-infant unity." It is only through the inevitable imperfection of fit between mother and infant that the "infant perceives that the source of his need associated with hunger, pain, and discomfort is within and the source of gratification is outside the self." This frustration provides the first opportunity for awareness of separateness.

This awareness of separateness, the movement from mother-infant unity to mother and infant (mother as now object) Ogden points out, implies the establishment of the psychological dialectic—of oneness and of separateness, wherein each creates and informs the other. The transitional object which now appears becomes a symbol for this separateness in unity, unity in separateness. It represents the infant (the omnipotently created extension of himself) and not the infant (the object/mother he has discovered that is outside of his omnipotent control). The appearance of a transitional object is not simply a milestone in the process of separation-individuation, but significantly, it reflects the beginning of a capacity to generate personal meanings and represent these in symbols, and according to Ogden, the beginning of a psychological dialectical process. "The attainment of the capacity to maintain psychological dialectics involves the transformation of the unity that did not require symbols into 'three-ness', a dynamic interplay of three differentiated entities. These entities are: the symbol (a thought), the symbolized (that which is being thought about), and the interpreting subject (the thinker generating his own thoughts and interpreting his own symbols). The differentiation of symbol, symbolized, and interpreting subject creates the possibility of potential space. That space between symbol and symbolized, mediated by an interpreting self, is the space in which creativity becomes possible. Within that space we can reflect on and make links between actions, feelings, and consequences so that our responses to others are intentional and not simply reflexive reactions to environmental provocations, such as we witnessed between Susie and her mother. It is therefore within this potential space that boundaries between self and others can be created.

A sense of the self, a sense of the other, and an intersubjective sense of the self with the other, a "wego" as Emde (1988) described it, can emerge from this potential space. Empathy is an aspect of this "wego," as within the potential space between mother and child each can "play with" the idea of being the other while at the same time knowing that one is not; by knowing that one is not the other, each can "play within" the relationship. As the child develops, the increasingly stable objective psychological boundaries between self and other that emerge from this potential space can also lead to increasing intimacy and maturity within meaningful relationships.

Establishing the objectivity for maintaining this dialectical process and potential space between self and other can be an ongoing developmental challenge for both child and parent. Defenses (such as projection, projective identification) which so frequently emerge in response to intense sexual or aggressive impulses, intense affects and the like, and often color perceptions of the other, threaten to collapse any potential space and the boundaries between self and object can become blurred, as was the case for both Susie and her mother, and for Colin, when he was angry at me. Success in maintaining an objective dialectic process is often dependent on the child's (and the parent's) capacity for self-regulation.

All modes of experiencing are called into play as a part of the child developing a capacity for self-regulation. Self-regulation begins with regulation within the attachment system. It also requires that the child identify with the regulating functions of the other as a part of the separation individuation process. Self-regulation also requires self-reflection, self-responsibility, mastery over feelings, desires, and impulses, and a capacity for flexible response. Owning and developing mastery over one's feelings, desires, and impulses requires some competence in containing them within manageable limits so that they do not disorganize and overwhelm self-regulatory functions. Self-regulation therefore also relies on the capacity to make use of the signaling function of affect.

The signaling function of an affect allows emotions to be used not only as part of a signaling system to and from others, but as a signal to the self. If an individual can recognize and reflect on an emotion before it disorganizes and overwhelms self-regulatory functions, the individual can mobilize a suitable plan. The emotional response can then be an adaptive one limited to manageable proportions. Being able to limit emotions to manageable proportions makes it easier to own an emotion, and maintain self and object boundaries (see Tyson, 2002, 2005 for elaboration of the signal function and its development).

If an individual has been unable to develop a capacity to use affects as signals and to maintain self-regulation, this signal function, sexual or aggressive instincts and emotional arousal cause distress and can lead to disorganization within the attachment system and/or within the "me" part of the ego/self system. The variety of pathological defenses that can be employed can result in a failure of maintaining the dialectical process, collapse of the potential space between parent and child, and collapse of objective self-object psychological boundaries. Boundary violations of various forms, the most egregious being child physical or sexual abuse, may then follow, indicating this collapse. The formation and maintenance of objective self-object boundaries therefore relies on affect regulation.

AFFECT REGULATION AND BOUNDARY FORMATION

In infancy and early childhood affects are automatic and peremptory in nature and easily disorganize immature regulatory functioning. Regulation therefore relies on the attachment system and its effectiveness for enhancing an infant's exploration and learning while ensuring emotional regulation and a sense of security (Sroufe, 1995). Repeated mutual exchanges with a caregiver who is sensitive to the infant's affective signals, thinks about how the infant might be feeling, mirrors and labels these affective states, and also intervenes before emotions become disorganizing gradually leads to the infant becoming aware of separateness. Differentiating from the sense of "twoness" to a "me" and "not me" world is an early form of a psychological dialectical process. "Finding" a transitional object indicates this differentiation and potential space is found between the two.

In the second year, signs of self-recognition appear. Declarations of "no," "mine," "me do it" herald a budding self-awareness. Expanding social narratives suggest that the toddler increasingly is consciously aware of a subjective sense of self and the relation of this subjective self to the rest of the world. A self-aware toddler is increasingly able to mentalize, to reflect on the subjective self, and he begins to recognizes that thoughts and feelings are lodged internally, in the mind, and that one can think about one's own thoughts and feelings as well as what is in the mind of the other. This of course makes the toddler increasingly aware that another person's actions may be driven by desires different from the child's own wishes (Fonagy, 2000). Complexity and challenge can then begin to characterize interactions. Power and control in the relationship may become a prevalent theme. The toddler tries, for example, to gain a sense of body ownership and independent body management, evident in wishes to feed herself, dress herself, and the like. Although usually messy and not very skilled in the beginning, a sense of competence comes from successful body management.

Efforts in self-expression also appear. Again, not very skilled in the beginning and with a limited repertoire and limited capacity for modulation, forceful self-expression in very young children is often awkward. Consequently, it is easily mistaken for aggression. The response of the environment usually determines what follows. The mother may respond with pleasurable reinforcement along with some gentle guidance to early attempts at self-assertion as well as some clear and consistent rules and expectations. Consistent expectations that are consistently enforced help the child feel safe—he knows what to expect. Safety within the relationship leads to an increasingly complex and mature relationship. Consistency within the relationship also facilitates the child, building secure inner structures in identification with the parental structure. Frustration tolerance, a regard for rules and expectations, and a sense of morality follow as the caregiver's rules and moral values gradually become those of the child. Self-discipline and self-esteem are enhanced, for these are built on success and reward, not punishment.

Of course, rules and expectations conflict with the desires of the child, and hateful feelings of protest and rage may erupt, the projection of which colors the perception of the caregiver. Maintaining safety and predictability during such times is a challenge to any caregiver. She must resist being drawn into angry protests and resist responding in kind or giving in. If the caregiver is able to maintain a distinction between her own emotions and those of the child, she is more able to contain, label, and reflect on the child's feelings, while remaining firm and consistent with her demands and expectations.

Creating a play space, engaging the child in symbolic play, can be very helpful during these times. On the day that Susie saw me as a monster, following her attempt to attack me she crawled under a chair and wailed. She was distraught and upset for quite some time, but eventually accepted my offer of reading her a story. Stories became a means for her to find safety, and eventually she began to act out the stories, changing the plot to meet her own internal reality. Playing contrasts with the child's inner psychic reality, and with the external world, and elements from each can be drawn into the play space. Symbolizing, labeling, and verbalizing thoughts and emotions through pretend play enable the child to elaborate the inner world of wishes, fears, feelings, and fantasies, and the outer world of rules and expectations, and to gain some control and mastery over the associated feelings.

If the caregiver can help the child create this "play space," and participate in ways that convey emotions to be meaningful and manageable, and label and reflect on the young child's experiences and emotional states, the child can begin to *use* the mother (Winnicott, 1969)—to discover that the mother is different from his projections and look to her to help him find flexible and adaptive ways of expressing and managing rage and other distressing affects, as well as ways of compromise and conflict resolution. In using the caregiver this way, the child gradually develops effective procedures for managing and regulating intense affects.

On the other hand, in response to the toddler's struggle for body owner-ship, self-assertion, and self-expression, a mother may feel provoked into a control battle. Responding to mother's restrictive words, gestures, and be-haviors, the toddler may erupt in rage. Struggles over willfulness, control, and body management may become intense. Anger is easily projected, and during a moment of rage the young child may see the mother as enraged, so that instead of a source of comfort and safety, mother becomes a feared per-secutor. The child easily feels desperately helpless, unloved, and over-whelmed with anxiety as well as rage as the child feels a loss of the loving and safe connection with the mother. These struggles make great demands on immature self-regulatory functions.

Great demands are also made on mother. One mother exclaimed, on de-scribing the challenges and tantrums of her three-year-old, "I feel like an an-gry three-year-old back; I feel like I want to kill her! I'm shocked, and I feel so guilty for feeling that angry! Sometimes it's really hard to maintain my per-spective."

At issue here is not merely the toddler's vicissitudes of development, but the mother's as well, for all of the developmental challenges mentioned have also been developmental challenges for the mother. Her own success or fail-ure in resolving these is reflected in her reaction to her child's independent and aggressive strivings. For although at times of stress the child may con-fuse object and subject, projected rage coloring perceptions of the mother, the mother ideally can make this differentiation and resist being drawn into the child's angry projections, and withstand provocation to respond in kind. However, the child's pattern of attachment usually reflects something of the mother's early attachment.

If issues of power, control, and body ownership remain, the parent may be easily provoked by the child's angry challenges. Projecting her own ag-gression onto the child, or displacing what she sees as her own bad self onto the child as a narcissistic extension of herself, she may see the child as an evil monster, a "bad seed." So frequently parents see the child and the child's body as a narcissistic extension of themselves, and behave as if they owned the child's body, and are entitled to invade it. Identifying with the child's pro-jections, the enraged parent blurs the boundary between parent and child, and may become verbally or physically abusive to the child; such inter-changes were frequently at issue between Susie and her mother.

Repetitive interactions of this kind can lead a child to become hypervigi-lant and hypersensitive (Perry et al., 1996). The child's projected rage, as well as her ability to provoke the parent's anger, has a double impact. As a fea-ture of the child's experience, it may produce overwhelming anxiety. Instead of the safety of a "holding environment," the person from whom the child seeks security becomes a source of fear, as we see in disorganized attachments. In addition, as the child forms an internal image of the parent, a frightening, persecuting, inner presence comes to provide a continuing internal source of anxiety (Ritvo, 1981). Then the image of the enraged persecuting parent, easily externalized, interferes with the child's "discovery" of different qualities of the actual parent or of a substitute caregiver who might be able to provide a source of safety and comfort. Self and object boundaries remain porous. In an environment where the child feels little safety, comfort, or reciprocal affective dialogue, the child also fails to develop a capacity for mentalization, and has no words with which to label feelings. This gives the child few tools with which to differentiate inner and outer reality, recognize links between intentions and actions, and between actions, consequences, and subsequent emotional states. Such children are often unable to engage in symbolic play, or their play can be concrete and repetitive. They do not make internal changes and compromises in response to conflict, or take responsibility for their actions. Instead, their actions are reflexive and are experienced as reactive impulses to environmental provocations, as they see themselves as passive victims of powerful external forces.

As development continues, and the wishes and increasingly complex conflicts of the infantile genital phase add additional challenges to self-regulatory functions, the extent to which self and object boundaries can be maintained may depend on earlier adaptations, and the use made of play space. An example is Jamie. Although originally loving and accepting of her baby sister, Jamie has become increasingly jealous. She recently said to her parents, "Mommy, Debbie is your baby, so I'm going to be Daddy's girl!" One night Jamie demands to stay up with Daddy for just one more television program. Mother empathizes with Jamie's wishes and with her disappointment, but reminds her that tomorrow is a school day; she must go to bed. Jamie, furious, says, "Mommy, I'm so mad at you, I'm going to send you and Debbie to the dungeon!" Mommy asks, but who will take care of Daddy? "I will of course! But don't you worry you'll never see him again!" After a little time of contemplation, seemingly confident in her mother's tolerance of her anger, she seeks rapprochement and figures out a way of "helping Mom" as she gets ready for bed.

Jamie is a child with a definitive sense of herself as agent; she sees herself as an intentional mental being who is able to own, take responsibility, and master her emotions by using imaginative play. Loewald maintains that the challenges of oedipal object relations represent a watershed in individuation. "The Oedipus Complex, with its basis in instinctual life, stands as a symbol in psychoanalytic psychology of the first delineation of man's love life beyond the empathic immersion of his environment, a symbol of the clear awakening of his life as an individual. It takes form through his passionate involvement, in love and hate, with his first libidinal objects, and through the limitations placed on this involvement which throw him back on himself." Loewald calls this "soul making."

CONCLUSION

I have suggested that we approach the task of understanding boundary formation by integrating the developmental perspectives of Bowlby, Mahler, and Winnicott. For this, I suggest we view the relative contribution of three modes of experiencing: experiencing from within the relationship or attachment system, experiencing the emerging and increasingly individuated sense of self, and experiencing the potential space between the two. I then described how self and object psychological boundaries might emerge from these modes of experiencing. Finally I described what I think are some of the important developmental processes, pathways, and stumbling blocks in the process of a young child negotiating these experiences which might enhance or interfere with their forming a firm sense of demarcation between self and other. Time does not allow us to further explore these processes through adolescence. However we should recognize that the adolescent process also makes a large contribution to an individual's final consolidation of an individuated self capable of maintaining emotional regulation and of assuming self-responsibility.

REFERENCES

Emde, R. (1988). Development terminable and interminable—1: Innate and motivational factors from infancy. *International Journal of Psychoanalysis* 69:23–42.

Fonagy, P. (2001). *Attachment Theory and Psychoanalysis.* New York: Other Press.

———, Gergely, G., Jurist, E., and Target, M. (2002). *Affect Regulation, Mentalization, and the Development of the Self.* New York: Other Press.

Freud, S. (1923). The ego and the id. *Standard Edition* 17:3–68.

Guntrip, H. (1969). *Schizoid Phenomena, Object Relations, and the Self.* New York: International Universities Press.

Loewald, H. (1979). The waning of the Oedipus complex. *Journal of the American Psychoanalytic Association* 27:751–775.

Ogden, T. (1985). On potential space. *International Journal of Psychoanalysis* 66:129–141.

Ritvo, S. (1981). Anxiety, symptom formation, and ego autonomy. *Psychoanalytic Study of the Child* 36:339–353.

Sroufe, L. A. (1995). *Emotional Development: The Organization of Emotional Life in the Early Years.* Cambridge: Cambridge University Press.

Tyson, P. (2002). Book review of *Affect Regulation, Mentalization, and the Development of the Self* by P. Fonagy, G. Gergely, E. Jurist, and M. Target. *Journal of the American Psychoanalytic Association* 50:628–637.

———. (2005). Affects, agency, and self-regulation. *Journal of the American Psychoanalytic Association* 53:159–187.

Winnicott, D. W. (1967). The mirror role of the mother and family in child development. In *Playing and Reality*, pp. 130–138. Middlesex, England: Penguin, 1971.

———. (1968). Playing: Its theoretical status in the clinical situation. *International Journal of Psychoanalysis* 9:591–599.

———. (1969). The use of an object. *International Journal of Psychoanalysis* 50:711–716.

———. (1971). *Playing and Reality*. Middlesex, England: Penguin.

3

Clinical Perspectives on the Development of Boundaries: Discussion of Tyson's Chapter, "Boundary Formation in Children: Normality and Pathology"

Ruth Garfield, M.D.

In her contribution, Dr. Phyllis Tyson reviews some of our developmental theories and extrapolates from them to focus upon the formation of boundaries. I will discuss her views and present my own thoughts about the development of boundaries around the self. However, before going into theoretical material, I will present the case of a young adult which will illustrate a failure in boundary formation.

THE CASE OF J

When I first met J she was a beginning junior at college. She was very attractive, appeared sultry, and spoke in a soft but husky voice. She was referred to me by a friend and colleague of mine in her home city. (She didn't know this woman but was close with her cousin who did.) Immediately she told me that she was on academic probation and was finding it very hard to concentrate. This had been going on for almost a year. She had done alright during her freshman year and very well in her highly competitive high school.

As we talked it was clear that the year had been more than academically challenging. In the previous summer she had begun regularly smoking marijuana and occasionally using cocaine. Her boyfriend from that summer (after freshman year) had been heavily into cocaine and convinced her to use it. Now, a year later, she was trying to extricate herself from that relationship; she only rarely used cocaine, but was still heavily into marijuana.

Very sadly and seriously, she explained that she found herself extremely anxious, especially in the morning, but suffered with anxiety all day. Attempts at studying made her feel lonely and desperate. To ease the loneliness and desperation, she would jog, go to yoga, at times attending a couple of yoga classes a day. She still talked frequently with the boy from the summer who wanted to continue the relationship with her. Repeatedly she told me she did not want to have a romantic, sexual relationship with him, but she couldn't say good-bye to anyone who had been in her life. Then she told me about the other people who had been in her life in the past year. There were several other men with whom she was involved; there were others with whom she had brief sexual affairs. There was also a boy on campus with whom she was flirting now.

As she talked about these men individually, she would describe the happiness and "closeness" she felt with each of them, what they offered her, and why it was so hard to think of giving each one up. She felt it was dishonest, immoral, to keep each relationship a secret, but other than that, she did not seem anxious or acknowledge anxiety as she would talk about them. Her felt anxiety was most pronounced around school issues.

I frequently found myself contracting the anxiety she denied. I felt anxious as she talked about these affairs. I wondered about my own anxiety about her apparent sexual and bodily freedom. Was I envious of her? Why was I feeling protective of her? I wondered if she was at least protecting herself physically from disease and pregnancy. Early on, I asked her about this, and she told me that she used protection. On one level she was taking care of herself. I was clearly feeling that she was also in danger of overexposure emotionally.

I listened to this story over the course of my first year of work with her. Gradually and gently, I began to raise with her the question of boundaries, and how she seemed to diminish or lose her sense of herself with other people. It seemed that she let people in too deeply and often didn't feel good about herself afterward. She talked more about how she was always anticipating what *they* wanted or needed from her; she could never say no. If someone told her he needed attention or care from her, emotionally or physically, she couldn't say no. She would see his needs as primary. When I asked her, she admitted that it was very hard to know what she wanted from others. She was amazed that I asked about this.

During that first year I heard very little about J's family. I knew that her father occasionally came down to see her, but rarely her mother. She said that her mother had been depressed and very "weird" since she was about eight, and mostly stayed in the house. There was a great-aunt, in her nineties, whom J visited as much as she could; she would cry as she talked about how much she loved her and feared her death. The aunt talked with her, gave her advice about life, and kissed and hugged her. Later, I heard more about her mother. For J, there was always a feeling that the mother had to be taken care of. She could not prepare the food her daughter wanted. "It's always what my mother wants and then she says it's my favorite thing to eat." My patient was never allowed to have sleepovers; she always had to stay close to home because "dangerous things" could happen if you wandered too far. She couldn't go out with friends until her late teenage years. Dating was prohibited. There was terrific conflict in the house between the parents. Interestingly, however, her very early years were unremembered.

I immediately thought about J when I was asked to talk about boundaries. I didn't yet know much about what had happened to interfere with the regulation of her boundaries, but something was clearly amiss with them.

SECURE YET PERMEABLE BOUNDARIES

In thinking about the concept of psychological boundaries, it occurs to me that here is a case of psychology recapitulating cytology. If, for example, we start with basic biology and examine the concept of boundaries at the cellular level, there are striking similarities. Each cell membrane contains the necessary contents of the cell, but in a nonrigid protective way. It is selectively permeable and permits the interior to remain intact while also serving as a barrier between the cell and its extracellular environment. There are several complex systems by which the cell gets what it needs and extrudes what it doesn't need or want.

When we speak of psychological boundaries demarcating the self, it is also most helpful to think in terms of a permeable but selective boundary, not one which is either totally porous or rigid. The infant is born into an environment which includes her caregiver. The baby's world with her caregiver begins the day she is born. According to contemporary theorists and infant researchers, such as Daniel Stern, the infant has a sense of emerging self which gradually develops into a core self and then a subjective/intersubjective self. There is a dynamic interaction with the caregiver from birth, although not a relationship of symbiosis or merger which implies a loss of self. Instead this early interaction is a necessary support and supplement to the growth of the infant. Robert Emde (1988) writes:

> A transactional perspective for early development now guides research. Accordingly, behavioral development is seen in terms of reciprocal relationships between the developing infant and the environment; new behaviors which result from this reciprocity, in turn, influence both infant and environment, and

such an iterative process continues as the complexity of organization increases. Thus individuality can be understood only in terms of "matches" between infant and environment and continuity can be understood only in terms of consistency of organism-environment (p. 27).

As I think about J I wonder about her earliest years. Despite the diagnosed but untreated depression (the mother refused treatment), I suspect that the mother's psychiatric problems were long standing and greatly frightening to J as a child. J had developed sense of self in her early years but without the benefit of consistent attunement and regulatory aid from her mother. She never had an opportunity to learn some of the needed rules of engagement, including those about boundary and affect regulation, and "social fitted-ness." She longed for and sought these things in her great-aunt, in her lovers, and eventually in me.

When deadlines or exam time approached, her anxiety heightened. Even though she was working so hard to curtail her sexual activity and mari-juana use, she searched for compromises. She asked me, "What if I just kissed him?" Or she would tell me that when she saw him, she asked for just a hug; "in that hug, for those few moments, my anxiety melted." She went through extended periods when she could not sleep. She said that if she could be held by someone she could sleep so peacefully, and in fact she would. She asked me to help her think of calming rituals to lessen her panic as bedtime approached. Eventually I gave her a prescription for a low-dose sleeping aid which she quartered. This was all she needed to sleep through the night and symbolically provided needed contact with me at these times.

I came to think that she was attempting to "merge" with these lovers and briefly lose herself and her anxiety. She wanted to melt away and be taken care of, the way she thought a baby might. This compulsion or longing to merge was also central to the overporosity of her boundaries.

Let me discuss the question of apparent merger or boundarylessness. From what I can gather, J's mother was not only inconstant for the ongoing emotional signaling that takes places between infant and caregiver; she was also unavailable for what Fred Pine calls moments of merger. This term is de-velopmentally apt. Although it does not endorse a necessary period of sym-biosis in development; it acknowledges that these *moments* may well take place and be necessary for the well-being of the infant and mother. While ac-knowledging that Mahler's original theory of the first two months of devel-opment as a symbiotic period does not fit current data or theory, Pine pro-poses that the infant has moments of the experience of "boundarylessness" or "merger." He writes, "My prime candidates for such moments of merger are those moments when the infant, in the mother's arms, having sucked vig-orously at breast or bottle progressively calms and falls into sleep as body tonus relaxes and he or she melts (J's word) into the mother's body" (1990, p. 238). He also believes this concept is supported by later life phenomena he divides into four categories:

1. panic-ridden experiences of dissolution (loss of boundaries)
2. delusional ideas of merger (which may or may not be accompanied by anxiety—which, in fact, may be blissful)
3. severe anxiety about separateness (in contrast to "oneness")
4. longings for merger (without experienced loss of boundaries) (1990, p. 233)

Pine also believes that these moments of merger of infantile experience are reconcilable with more contemporary research on the aware, cognitive infant with a self or emerging self.

Stern, on the other hand, argues that despite the feeling state imagined in the infant and experienced by the caregiver, each maintains their core self, and there is no confusion about who is doing or feeling what. His belief is that the sense of merger is illusory.

Whether or not true merger or boundarylessness occurs emotionally, the feelings and longings obviously have clinical relevance. Certainly Pine's descriptions resonate with my understanding of J. This concept, especially the longing for merger, may be helpful in understanding more about what gets some clinicians into boundary trouble.

Pine's search for momentary mergerlike experiences in adult life led him to identify just one, orgasm. I think there are more such moments in one's life. Romantic love or intense feelings toward your child exemplify this. Friends and I have confided about that unspeakably intense feeling when you feel "in love with your child." There are moments when you "lose yourself" to uncontrolled laughter, perhaps akin to orgasm. There are experiences of spiritual moments of union or creative moments when one loses oneself. So I think that Pine is onto something here in early development that needs further thought. These experiences are positive and pleasurable, feel close to merger, but do not feel threatening to the self.

ARE THERE CLINICAL MOMENTS OF MERGER?

In the clinical situation, even when boundaries are being carefully considered, there are moments when the boundaries of patient and therapist seem to match up in terms of their selective permeability, in a way that may feel like a fleeting moment of merger. This may occur for the purpose of sending emotional signals or important communications. This transfer between therapist and patient reminds me of the necessary flow across boundaries that occurs between caregivers and infants (and as in the cell membrane). Very carefully the therapist tries to find the channels to make a foray into the psyche of the other but then, importantly and necessarily, moves back out.

These moments are crucial to psychotherapy and to how I understand treatment with patients. Many patients enter psychotherapy with a readiness to let in the therapist. Despite the resistance and defenses they present, they often possess a longing to be understood and known; they may be all too willing to surrender power and have us permeate their boundaries. Jessica Benjamin (1994) writes:

> The aspect of erotic transference I want to address here has to do with the analyst as the bestower if recognition—the one who knows, or could know, the patient. To be known or recognized is immediately to experience the other's power. The other becomes the one who can give or withhold recognition; who can see what is hidden; who can reach, conceivably even violate, the core of the self. This attribution of the power to know is closely bound up with erotic experience in general, but I suspect that it forms the kernel of the erotic transference (pp. 538–539).

The confusion between erotic longing and yearning to be known becomes applied to lovers, parents, and other authority figures, including analysts and therapists. Boundaries of body and psyche are inherently then quite vulnerable, when the longing to be "known" has gone unfulfilled, and appropriated only to another, rather than the self. The goal of treatment is knowledge of one's self in the context of another, the analyst, but eventually by oneself. This requires mastery of boundaries and the temptations to violate them. Benjamin writes further:

> The freedom from internal and external constraint of the object, floating in the reflection of the other's knowledge, which need not be distinguished from the self's knowledge, informs the erotics of the intersubjective space. This experience of being known generates a profound sense of love, but it is love of self and other at the same time, not of one at the expense of the other. This erotics of transference does differ from the well-known erotic transference, the genitally charged passion of falling in love with the powerful analyst, the seduction of which inevitably compromises the sense of self (p. 554).

With J, I have, of course, tried to be very careful about boundaries. That does not mean that I am rigid. After nine months of treatment, she was moving to an apartment farther from my office. She thought about finding someone else to see. She complained that I did not say enough, although she was clear that she was feeling much better in terms of her anxiety. Instead of twice a week she proposed a longer session once a week. I decided to try it with her. I also listened to what she was saying in terms of my talking. She needed more than my mirroring face or attunement to her affect. As she talked more about her parents and the relationship with her mother, I made more connections which she found extremely helpful. As soon as she began to identify and understand her intense longing for closeness (merger?) as a substitute for what she didn't get in a house where there were no hugs and kisses, she began to think about limiting her romantic/sexual involvements—the beginning of a long process.

We talk a lot about boundaries, about what she longs for and is angry not to have received. I talk with her about not having received help with regulation of the boundaries. I feel she has begun to engage in what Emde calls social referencing with me. Emde (1988) writes that this is a "process whereby a person of any age seeks out emotional information from a significant other in order to make sense of a situation that is otherwise uncertain or ambiguous" (p. 31). We've also begun to talk more about her anger and rage which she had said she almost never felt. She will laugh though as she thinks about how prohibitive her mother was and how her mother would react if she only knew more about her life. Her laughter, however, belies her anger, sadness, and longing to be known by her mother.

DEVELOPMENT OF BOUNDARIES AND MORALITY

The notion of "boundaries" is a psychological concept with inherent ties to moral behavior, as much as we tend not to want to think in those terms. There are "rules" about how to treat the boundaries of others and ourselves. This is clearer to us when they've been trespassed. In our field we so rarely want to declare that something is good or bad. That I believe reflects our own difficulties with boundaries.

When I meet with parents of a child that I have been treating, and they tell me about regularly screaming at a child to the point that they "lose it," I feel obliged to comment on their overstepping a boundary. Dr. Tyson is correct in her labeling verbal abuse a boundary violation and destructive; the child feels often overwhelmed as if someone who loves them has reached in, without their permission, to knock the boundaries down. As she points out, parents need to have mastered the developmental task of self-responsibility to help their children regulate boundaries. In the midst of a child's provocations, a parent must struggle with their own intense feelings stirred up in response. Only in that way can the boundary between parent and child be maintained, but a respect for boundaries can be conveyed even during conflict.

In my mother-baby group, one 18-month-old boy would suddenly stop his play and go around to kiss the others in the group. Of course the adults thought this was adorable, but then he approached the one-year-old baby girl. For a moment she startled, looked over at her mother, and then began to cry. Perhaps she had heard a loud noise from construction, we said. Then the same sequence occurred again later in the group. Stefan kissed everyone and Sara burst into tears. He was too unknown for her and too close. The next week his mother, who is quite affectively tuned in, talked to the group about having spoken with Stefan about kissing and hugging only people in the family or when people say it's okay. At the next group, he appeared much more thoughtful and solemn until the end, when his mother said it was okay to hug some of us.

It's interesting to me that Emde turns his attention to moral behavior in his paper on infant motivation. After reviewing the research he believes rules have a "basis in innate organized structures" and that these "internalized rules are entitled to be considered as early moral motives having a dual origin in inborn propensity and caregiver relationship experience" (1988, p. 32). In studies with preschool children, it has been shown that even before there is language, there seem to be rules about how to engage in play, maintain, and stop it (implying boundaries). There seems to be an inherent sense of taking turns and even the Golden Rule. The research indicates that although the baby has in place the foundation for moral behavior, the presence of an affectively attuned caregiver is critical to its development. This was seen with Stefan and his mother, and by its absence in J.

Finally, Emde describes an experiment with three-year-olds which demonstrates the significance of parental attunement on moral development. A mother leaves the child and researcher in the room after showing him two new toys, but with the injunction that they not be played with now. After a few minutes, the researcher picks up a puppet who, in play mode, suggests they play with those very toys. The child most often says, "Didn't you hear my mommy. We can't play with those." Emde writes, "We came to a startling realization. These children had developed an executive sense of 'we', of the significant other being with them, which gave them an increased sense of power and control" (p. 35).

In our work as therapists, we become the "other" in the "we." When patients such as J present with developmental problems in boundary formation, the need to monitor closely our own boundaries and those of the patient is crucial. By reflecting more about this as a useful developmental and therapeutic concept, I hope we can understand more fully both the need for and cautions in the "we-ness" or "wego" (Emde, 1988) of appropriate clinical boundaries.

CONCLUSION

In conclusion, the consideration of boundaries as a psychological construct is timely and important. At a time when we are thinking more about the relational aspects of our work as psychoanalysts and psychotherapists, it is important to examine in depth these kinds of interactive concepts. We can begin to see that the notion of boundaries has a developmental line that is interwoven with that of self-responsibility and morality. There are also important technical and therapeutic implications and significant moral ones for incorporating a greater awareness of the concept of boundaries into our work.

REFERENCES

Benjamin, J. (1994). What angel would hear me?: The erotics of transference. *Psychoanalytic Inquiry* 14:535–557.

Coates, S. (1998). Having a mind of one's own and holding the other in mind: Commentary on paper by Peter Fonagy and Mary Target. *Psychoanalytic Dialogues* 8(1):115–148.

Emde, R. (1988). Development terminable and interminable—1. Innate and motivational factors from infancy. *International Journal of Psychoanalysis* 69:23–42.

Pine, F. (1990). *Drive, Ego, Object, and Self: A Synthesis for Clinical Work.* New York: Basic.

———. (1992). Some refinements of the separation-individuation concept in light of research on infants. *Psychoanalytic Study of the Child* 47:103–116.

Stern, D. (1985). *The Interpersonal World of the Infant.* New York: Basic.

Tyson, P., and Tyson, R. (1990). *Psychoanalytic Theories of Development: An Integration.* New Haven, CT: Yale University Press.

4

Sexual and Nonsexual Boundary Violations in Psychoanalysis and Psychotherapy

Glen Gabbard, M.D.

Boundaries in the analytic setting have two connotations. The term is often used to describe the architecture of the analytic frame—the elements that comprise the envelope in which the treatment takes place. These dimensions might include such things as the place in which appointments are arranged; a fee that is paid to the analyst, recognizing that a fiduciary relationship exists; confidentiality; asymmetry of self-disclosure; a specific time in which the work of the analysis occurs; abstention from sexual relations; and limits on other forms of physical contact

When one discusses boundaries of psychoanalytic technique, one enters into another realm with a related but different connotation. The term is also used to define the limits of "widening scope" technique. One must be cautious in trying to apply analytic technique to patients who require more ego-supportive interventions. The interface of the two connotations of boundaries leads us into a fundamental paradox—namely, that radical departures from the analytic frame are rationalized in the treatment of highly disturbed and traumatized patients—exactly those patients who require a containing but clear "boundedness" to avoid the retraumatization and boundarylessness of childhood.

In this chapter, I will describe how analytic boundaries are often eroded by a variety of intersubjective factors involving characteristics of the patient and the analyst. I will focus particularly on those analysts and therapists who are essentially ethical individuals who are drawn into complicated transference-countertransference enactments with one particular patient under a unique set of circumstances.

A flexible frame has long been recognized as necessary for patients who have greater deficits and require interventions other than interpretation (Gedo, 1993, Gabbard and Lester, 2003). Indeed, analytic boundaries are established physically so they can be crossed psychologically. To establish a connection that is meaningful and empathic, analysts must vary boundaries with different patients and even with the same patient across sessions. Mitchell (1993) once noted that "what is most crucial is neither gratification nor frustration, but the process of negotiation itself, in which the analyst finds his own particular way to confirm and participate in the patient's subjective experience yet, over time, establishes his own presence and perspective in a way that the patient can find enriching rather than demolishing" (p. 196).

Greenberg (1995) also stressed that the analyst's subjectivity is a key factor in establishing a flexible frame, in that some analysts by nature are more self-disclosing, for example, than are others. Some require greater degrees of privacy or lesser degrees of spontaneity. However one negotiates the particular analytic boundaries with a given patient, there is an understanding that these boundaries serve the function of creating an analytic object. The relative asymmetry in the dyad and the peculiarities of the frame allow for the emergence of a transference object or series of objects that can be analyzed and interpreted. The analyst's subjectivity cannot be excluded from the equation, and therefore one might view the analytic object as a joint creation of the interpenetrating subjectivities of the two participants (Gabbard and Lester, 2003). Both the real characteristics of the analyst and the internalized object relations of the patient come together in this amalgam, reflecting something similar to the decentered subject that Ogden refers to as the "analytic third" (1994).

A contemporary's perspective on analytic theory and technique would acknowledge that countertransference enactments are inevitable and therefore will create minor versions of boundary transgressions throughout the treatment (Gabbard, 1995; Renik, 1993). Hence we can differentiate between boundary crossings and boundary violations (Gutheil and Gabbard, 1993, 1998). Boundary violations are generally regarded as egregious enactments, such as sexual relations with a patient, that are repetitive, pervasive, and harmful to the patient as well as destroying the viability of the analytic treatment. They often are not subjected to analytic scrutiny, so they exist outside of the analytic work. One analyst, for example, told his patient that they did not need to talk about the hugging and kissing between them because they were part of the "real relationship." By contrast, boundary crossings are benign and even helpful countertransference enactments that are attenuated—i.e., the analyst catches herself in the process of enacting something and reflects on it. They are more likely to occur in isolation, are subject to analytic scrutiny, and extend the analytic work in a positive direction.

In this regard, one must avoid assuming a rigid posture to avoid analytic boundary violations and therefore drain the analytic work of spontaneous and flexible reactions to the patient. Ideally, analysts must simultaneously participate in the "dance" presented by the patient while also reflecting on what is transpiring (Gabbard, 1995).

VULNERABLE THERAPISTS

In my experience with over 150 cases of boundary-violating therapists where I have been involved as a consultant, evaluator, or treater, I have learned that there is no simple formula that can be used to characterize therapists who commit boundary violations. A variety of different types of professionals engage in boundary violations for a myriad of reasons. By far the most common gender constellation where sexual relations occur is a male therapist and female patient. Large samples suggest, however, that about 20% involve female therapists and 20% involve same-sex dyads (Schoener et al., 1989).

From a practical standpoint, all therapists should consider themselves vulnerable to serious boundary violations, particularly under certain kinds of stress. A divorce, a serious illness in a family member, death of a parent or a spouse, or a suicide of a patient are all examples of stressors that may lead therapists who are ordinarily ethical into states of desperate neediness where the patient appears to offer some salvation from a state of despair. The natural tendency of therapists and analysts is to assume that serious boundary violations only occur to impaired colleagues who are different than they are. Unfortunately, this projective disavowal makes them less likely to monitor their own work with an eye to enactments that may foreshadow more egregious transgressions. The wisest and most practical approach is to assume that boundary violations are an occupational hazard that may occur in the course of anyone's career.

I have found it useful to think about boundary-violating therapists as falling into one of four categories in the following psychoanalytically based classification (Gabbard and Lester, 2003): (1) psychotic disorders, (2) predatory psychopathy, (3) lovesickness, and (4) masochistic surrender. I do not mean to suggest that all cases fall neatly into these categories. Some analysts and therapists fall between the cracks or have elements of more than one category. However, these groupings help one to think about the potential for rehabilitation and return to productive practice. I would like to particularly focus on the last two groups, in which essentially honest and competent therapists are brought into serious problems with particular patients. These two categories may encompass a variety of diagnostic entities, ranging from milder forms of narcissistic personality to depressive states to neurotically organized colleagues. Some analysts and therapists may be essentially normal but under great stress, while others may have longstanding characterological problems related to early trauma.

COMMON THEMES

A set of common themes emerges in the evaluation and treatment of these individuals. One of these themes is a type of omnipotence wherein the therapist believes "only I can save the patient." This omnipotent fantasy often leads to extraordinary rescue efforts where one boundary is violated after another until the descent down the slippery slope is irrevocable.

Another common theme is one I have termed "disidentification" with the aggressor (Gabbard, 1997, 2003). In the analytic treatment of patients who have experienced severe childhood trauma, the posture of the analyst may be a desperate attempt to disavow any connection with the internalized bad object who is responsible for the abuse. The analyst may feel invaded by the abusive object and may unconsciously identify with it. In a desperate effort to deny aggression, the analyst unwittingly escalates heroic efforts to rescue the patient, ultimately leading to a retraumatization of the patient by transgressing the ordinary boundaries of the analytic frame.

Analysts and therapists may also reenact their own childhood trauma with patients. The ethical proscription against sexual relations between analyst and patient may intensify longings in the lovesick analyst in the same way that the forbidden nature of the oedipal situation fuels the longings in the child. When a lovesick male analyst begins to disclose his personal problems to a younger female patient, interlocking enactments of rescue fantasies may emerge. The female patient may have harbored a childhood fantasy that she was somehow taking care of her depressed father in despair over an empty marriage. The analyst, on the other hand, may be unconsciously rescuing his depressed mother in his attempt to heal the patient. Female patients who have suffered childhood trauma may be particularly appealing to the lovesick analyst who is intent on rescue. Male analysts may misinterpret a longing for maternal nurturance as a sexual overture at a genital developmental level and respond accordingly. Patients in such situations may ambivalently comply with the analyst's overtures because they are accustomed to expect a sexual relationship in association with the caring they receive.

Under the guise of lovesick feelings for the patient, a great many aggressive and sadistic feelings may emerge. Professions of love may be designed to heal the patient through a reparenting process rather than through a systematic understanding of the patient's internal world. The more the analyst fears she has fallen in love with the patient, the more aggression is submerged and disavowed so that insidiously it works its way into a corruption of the analytic process. As Mitchell noted in 1997, "Aggression is love's shadow, an inextricable accompaniment and necessary constituent of romantic passion" (p. 31).

Steiner (2000) once noted that our love for analysis is constantly threatened by our unconscious hatred of analysis. Analysts may experience the role as confining and restraining to the point that they wish to throw off the shackles of analytic constraint and try to provide the patient with something he or she did not receive in childhood. Ferenczi, for example, noted that he was trying to give his patients what he himself did not receive from his mother (Dupont, 1988). Hence there may be an envy of the patient's position. The patient receives the full attention provided by the holding environment of the analytic setting while the analyst is feeling relatively deprived, especially if there are stressors in the analyst's life outside that lead to feelings of deprivation and longing.

A perception of deficit is also a key factor in many serious boundary violations. The analyst may be convinced that a deficit state requires an effort to fill the deficit through extraordinary measures rather than to use ordinary analytic understanding, while ignoring the presence of internal conflict. This attempt to fill a deficit may take a concretized form of filling the vagina with the analyst's penis.

In other cases, it may simply be reflected in the analyst's attempt to be an unconditionally loving parent to repair the damage from childhood by an abusive parent. A clinical example will illustrate some of these themes. I have deliberately chosen a female analyst in that the vast majority of the literature involves accounts of male therapists, once again leaving the female psychology a bit of a "dark continent."

THE CASE OF DR. F

Dr. F was a female analyst in her fifties who came to see me for a consultation. With barely controlled emotion in her voice, she told me she was on the verge of losing her mind. She explained that she was "stuck" with a patient. She gave a harrowing account of her treatment of Cathy, a chronically suicidal 29-year-old patient she had seen for a period of 10 months. Cathy originally saw Dr. F after a six-month sexual relationship with her male therapist ended. She was intent on killing herself but first wanted to give treatment with Dr. F a try. She told Dr. F that she had had incestuous sexual relations with her father and had a lifelong conviction that she was a bad person as a result. According to Cathy, her mother had known about the incest, but felt that it was helpful for her daughter to take over the responsibility of satisfying her husband's sexual needs since she was chronically exhausted taking care of the house and the children.

Cathy told Dr. F that she had purchased a gun and was intending to use it on her 30th birthday, which was seven months away. Dr. F felt a chill run down her spine. A month prior to her first meeting with Cathy, she had lost another patient to suicide. She thought to herself that she could not bear to go through that experience again. She had even considered leaving the profession and retiring early. She tried to transfer Cathy to a colleague, but Cathy's response was, "No one will want me now I'm damaged goods," referring to the sexual relationship she had had with her previous therapist.

Cathy told Dr. F that suicide was on her mind all the time. Although she had not actually attempted suicide, she felt it was only a matter of time. Dr. F felt she had to do everything in her power to prevent the suicide. Part of her felt that this was a chance to redeem herself for the previous suicide, for which she blamed herself. Another part of her wanted to get rid of Cathy, but she feared that abandoning her would precipitate a suicide.

She embarked on a course of three-times-weekly treatment, even though Cathy could barely afford it. Dr. F lowered her fee dramatically. Much of the content revolved around horrific abuse and neglect in Cathy's family of origin, and Dr. F thought that only some version of reparenting would save Cathy from her own hand. Dr. F told me that she was influenced by Loewald and Winnicott, both of whom viewed psychoanalysis as having much in common with parenting. She also knew she had little time until the patient's 30th birthday and felt pressured to provide a loving relationship that would make Cathy feel like life was worth living.

Using Margaret Little's account of her treatment with Winnicott to justify her strategy, she held the patient's hand, and told her that she loved her. But the patient continued to talk about suicide in every session. Cathy told Dr. F that her professions of love seemed hollow because she was paid to say that. She said she had been deceived before by therapists and did not trust her. Cathy went on to say that she was running out of money and could no longer see Dr. F anyway. Dr. F promised that she would see her for free.

To assure Cathy that her love was real, Dr. F hugged her tightly at the end of each session. These hugs were extremely gratifying to Cathy, and she told Dr. F, "When you hug me, it's like a narcotic has been injected into my veins. I'm getting addicted to them. I can't do without them. It gives me reason to live."

As will happen with all addictive drugs, Cathy soon developed tolerance to the hugs and wanted something more from her therapist. Dr. F took Cathy on shopping trips with the rationale that she would be providing the kind of mother-daughter relationship that Cathy had never experienced. During these trips, she would frequently buy Cathy articles of clothing, and they would go to restaurants to have a bite to eat. At times they would go to a movie after a day of shopping, and Cathy told her that for the first time in her life, she felt like she had a mother who loved her. Cathy told Dr. F that she wanted her to be her *real* mother. But Dr. F explained that the best she could do was to be *like* a mother.

Cathy felt spurned. Her feeling of rejection heightened when Dr. F said she could not see her during an upcoming weekend because her daughter, who lived in another city, would be visiting her. Cathy was enraged at the thought of someone taking her place. She went to Dr. F's house and watched through a window as Dr. F made dinner with her daughter. She became furious and called Dr. F on her cell phone. Dr. F told her that she needed her privacy. Cathy's response was, "Fine I'll kill myself then." Dr. F begged her not to act on the impulses and to come to her office first thing in the morning.

Cathy appeared at the office, and Dr. F apologized profusely for being so abrupt with her the night before. She explained to the patient that she had had a suicide in her practice not long ago, and could not go through that experience again. Cathy proposed a bargain—if they could spend at least one day together each weekend, she would not commit suicide. Dr. F told her she could not agree to the bargain because she needed some personal space. She explained that Cathy had taken over her private life, and she needed to have other relationships as well. She suggested that they confine their meetings to the three therapy sessions a week. She also said they had to stop the hugs because they were making her worse. Cathy screamed at her: "You can't expect me to go cold turkey Your hugs are my medication. You can't turn back the clock. You can't give me something, and then take it away."

Having heard this saga, I asked Dr. F if she had thought of hospitalizing the patient so she could get the benefit of a treatment team working with her around how to extricate herself from the relationship. She explained that Cathy refused hospitalization and threatened to report her to her licensing board if she tried to commit her. She said that she would tell everyone about Dr. F's unethical behavior and ruin her career. Dr. F felt that she was being held hostage and had no choice but to continue seeing her three times a week in her office and spend a weekend day with her outside the office, even though both of them seemed miserable much of the time.

I asked Dr. F how she had gotten herself into the current situation in the first place. She explained that she had grown up with a suicidal mother, and on more than one occasion had observed her mother sitting in the basement with a gun in her lap, contemplating suicide. She said that those experiences had made her decide to become a therapist and try to help people who were in such despair. She was unable to save her mother from ultimately killing herself, but she felt she had to save her patients from suicide. Dr. F told me the patient was driving her crazy and she was desperate to find a way out.

DISCUSSION

This case is typical of those that I have categorized as masochistic surrender. Dr. F was not in love with the patient. However, she felt bullied into surrendering to the patient's demands as a way of preventing suicide. As I have noted in other contributions (Gabbard, 2003), this variation of boundary violation often occurs as part of the mismanagement of the suicidal patient, particularly if the patient is a childhood abuse victim. In this case, Cathy was also the victim of sexual exploitation by a previous therapist as well.

Dr. F clearly was attempting to disidentify with the aggressor and disavow any connection with Cathy's internal representation of an abusive or neglectful object, whether mother, father, or previous therapist. We can appreciate the frame of mind in which she began the treatment of Cathy and understand that there is something of ourselves that prefers to avoid the negative transference, particularly in the context of her recent loss of a patient by suicide. Dr. F attempted to provide an unconditionally loving parental experience by making herself available to the patient on weekends, hugging the patient, and even treating the patient as if she were a child.

One reason this strategy fails is that the patient is searching for a "bad enough" object (Rosen, 1993; Gabbard, 2000). If we do not allow ourselves to be transformed into the bad object role, the patient will need to continue to escalate demands until we become so exasperated that we begin to "lose our minds" as Dr. F did, and tell the patient how angry we are and how we cannot go on anymore in the effort to be a real parent.

Dr. F's situation also represents another common theme in the serious boundary violations—namely, a particular fit between the internal world of the patient and the internal world of the analyst. Dr. F was particularly vulnerable to disidentifying with the aggressor because of her private concern that she had failed her previous patient and had therefore contributed to the patient's suicide. In her heart, she believed she had killed the previous patient. She wanted to do whatever she could to prove she was not a murderer. Moreover, Dr. F's childhood had been haunted by an attempt to talk her mother out of suicide. Dr. F's anxiety about the potential for Cathy to kill herself was readily detected by Cathy, who then knew the buttons she had to push to ensure that her therapist would respond to her needs. Dr. F told me that she had been overly concerned about the suicidal ideas and intent by Cathy, and that every time they met she would try to talk Cathy out of feeling suicidal.

Dr. F's anxiety about whether or not the patient might act compromised her ability to think clearly and reflectively about the meaning of Cathy's suicidality. She had a failure of mentalization that paralleled the patient's failure. Cathy did not view Dr. F "as if" she were an idealized mother—she literally wanted her to be a mother to her. In a similar vein, Dr. F, in a collapse of the analytic space, treated Cathy as though heroic action involving her enactment of the role of an actual mother was the only thing that would save her (Gabbard, 2003). Her own sense of a play space needed for treatment got lost in a flurry of concern about what concrete action should be taken to prevent the suicide. Moreover, by concretely encouraging the patient to think of her as a real parent who is always available, Dr. F set herself up for disaster. This implied promise filled the patient with false hopes that ultimately had to be dashed.

PREVENTION

The goal of preventing boundary violations has a quixotic dimension to it. There is a radical privacy to psychoanalysis and psychotherapy that creates a unique vulnerability. We will never be able to prevent all cases of destructive exploitation of patients. Education and a personal analytic experience for all practitioners are helpful, but limited. We analysts are masters of self-deception. No matter how thoroughly we understand boundary violations, no matter how extensive our personal analytic experiences may be, we can convince ourselves that our departures from the frame are in the best interests of the patient and are manageable because of our experience and knowledge of psychoanalytic work.

Hence by far the best preventive measure is regular consultation with a colleague or a group of colleagues. However, forces within our field conspire against this practice. We have a peculiar notion of autonomy in our field. We are trained in the context of a triad of patient, analyst, and supervisor. When we graduate, though, we are thrust into the cold on our own and expected to fly solo. The analytic dyad has an incestuous quality to it. Two people interact behind a locked door without the knowledge of a third party. The introduction of a consultant introduces a "third" that is crucial to disrupting the incestlike quality of the dyad.

We are also trained to compartmentalize what happens in the office and keep it apart from the rest of our psyche. If we hear confidential information about a colleague from the couch, we know we cannot use it. So we sequester it in a private compartment in an effort to assure that it won't enter into casual conversation when gossiping with friends and colleagues. Hence we can easily start down the slippery slope when we begin sequestering what we are actually doing with patients so that colleagues will not tell us to stop or to change our technical approach. All candidates must be taught that if there is anything they are doing that they would not feel comfortable telling a supervisor or consultant, they are in trouble. They need to contact a consultant and tell all before disaster strikes.

Finally, we must also attend to the powerful group forces that operate in psychoanalytic organizations to prevent seeing what is before our eyes.

Massive denial of boundary violations and their impact have been our historical legacy (Gabbard and Peltz, 2001). We tend to protect each other. We also are more likely to want to understand the dynamic themes in transgressions than to say to a colleague: "Cut it out." To preserve the integrity of psychoanalysis, we must have the courage to be nonanalytic at times.

REFERENCES

Dupont, J., ed. (1988). *The Clinical Diary of Sandor Ferenczi* (trans. M. Balint and M. G. Jackson). Cambridge, MA: Harvard University Press.

Gabbard, G. O. (1995). Countertransference: The emerging common ground. *International Journal of Psychoanalysis* 76:475–485.

———. (1997). Challenges in the analysis of adult patients with histories of childhood sexual abuse. *Canadian Journal of Psychoanalysis* 5:1–25.

———. (2000). On gratitude and gratification. *Journal of the American Psychoanalytic Association* 48:698–716.

———. (2003). Miscarriages of psychoanalytic treatment in suicidal patients. *International Journal of Psychoanalysis* 84:249–261.

———, and Lester, E. (2003). *Boundaries and Boundary Violations in Psychoanalysis*. Washington, DC: American Psychiatric Press.

Gabbard, G. O., and Peltz, M. (2001). Speaking the unspeakable: Institutional reactions to boundary violations by training analysts. *Journal of Applied Psychoanalysis* 49:659–673.

Gedo, J. U. (1993). *Beyond Interpretation: Toward a Revised Theory for Psychoanalysis* (Revised Edition). Hillsdale, NJ: Analytic Press.

Greenberg, J. R. (1995). Psychoanalytic technique and the interactive matrix. *Psychoanalytic Quarterly* 64:1–22.

Gutheil, T. G., and Gabbard, G. O. (1993). The concept of boundaries in clinical practice: Theoretical enriched management dimensions. *American Journal of Psychiatry* 150:188–196.

———. (1998). Misuses and misunderstandings in boundary theory in clinical and regulatory settings. *American Journal of Psychiatry* 155:409–414.

Mitchell, S. A. (1993). *Hope and Dread in Psychoanalysis*. New York: Basic.

———. (1997). Psychoanalysis and the degradation of romance. *Psychoanalytic Dialogues* 7:23–42.

Ogden, T. H. (1994). *Subjects of Analysis*. Northvale, NJ: Jason Aronson.

Renik, O. (1993). Analytic interaction: Conceptualizing technique in light of the analyst's irreducible subjectivity. *Psychoanalytic Quarterly* 62:553–571.

Rosen, I. (1993). Relational masochism: The search for a bad-enough object. Presented to the Topeka Psychoanalytic Society, January 21.

Schoener, G. R., Milgrom, J. H., Gonsiorek, J. C., Luepker, E. T., and Conroe, R. M. (1989). *Psychotherapists' Sexual Involvement with Clients: Intervention and Prevention*. Minneapolis, MN: Walk-In Counseling Center.

Steiner, J. (2000). Book review of *A Mind of One's Own: A Kleinian View of Self and Object* by R. Caper. *Journal of the American Psychoanalytic Association* 48:637–643.

5

Going over the Edge—
A One-Person or Two-Person
Psychology? Discussion of
Gabbard's Chapter, "Sexual and
Nonsexual Boundary Violations in
Psychoanalysis and Psychotherapy"

Ira Brenner, M.D.

We are indebted to Dr. Gabbard for the enduring contributions he has made in furthering our understanding of boundary violations in the psychotherapies. His developmental perspective and appreciation of the evolution of analytic thinking about the whole concept of boundaries provides a framework from which we can examine the multitude of variables that are operative when such breaches occur. I agree with his formulation and recommendations in the case he presented of Dr. F's masochistic surrender to her seductive patient Cathy. Confronted with the enormous pressure of an imminently suicidal patient, we clinicians may resort to heroic measures to try to save someone we deem untreatable under ordinary conditions. But even if this determination of untreatability were true, an underlying, grandiose, messianic fantasy in the therapist may result in a potentially lethal collision of psyches. Especially in therapists where unresolved mourning is present, as was the case with Dr. F, unconscious guilt and fantasies of reviving the dead may fuel therapeutic zeal. In addition to seeking consultation, one must also consider visiting one's analyst again for however long it takes to work through the issues and "recalibrate" (Isakower, 1938), as it were.

As Dr. Gabbard points out, contemporary analytic views of mental functioning and analytic technique both broaden our domain and increase our risks. In this context, I would like to consider how the extremes of technique from the early Freudian notion of the uninvolved, unflappable surgeon (Freud, 1912) to the experimental, mutual analyses described by Ferenczi (1932) could represent absurd ends of a continuum of a one-person to a two-person psychological approach. At one end, there would be so little emotional involvement by the analyst that the risk of a boundary violation would be very low, whereas at the other end the mutual free associations, disclosures, and revelations of sexual fantasies and even taking turns using the couch, by its very nature, blurs the psychic boundaries in the dyad. Given the problematic history of boundary problems in some of our famous psychoanalytic forefathers, the risks of overinvolvement with patients is a sobering accompaniment to the enormous challenges facing us as clinicians. These challenges are further increased by those enactment-prone patients whose own development was marred by impingements, violations, and other interferences with the integration of their minds and bodies. As Freud ruefully observed after his ill-fated treatment of Dora, a young victim of her father's friend's lust, "No one who, like me, conjures up the most evil of those half-tamed demons that inhabit the human breast and seeks to wrestle with them can expect to come through the struggle unscathed" (1905, p. 109). Given the fact that we usually associate boundary violations with sexual transgressions, it is important not to lose sight of the role of aggression in such cases, as Freud implies.

In the following case which led to a disaster, a woman prone to "fatal attractions" (Kales, 2003) was under the care of a predator-type clinician (Gabbard and Lester, 1995). She had a diagnosis of a very severe dissociative disorder (DID) and a history of early neglect and sexual trauma. After presenting this clinical material, I will briefly review recent findings in developmental research which support a dyadic, interpersonal origin of dissociation and describe how her exploitation took advantage of this underlying vulnerability. I will then argue that the therapeutic process with such patients requires a consideration of both relational and intrapsychic factors.

CASE REPORT

Many years ago and in what now feels like a foreign land, it was possible to treat very disturbed patients in the hospital for extended periods of time. Mrs. V, a woman in her thirties, lived in an underserved area and traveled a great distance for a series of hospitalizations under my care, for up to a year in duration over a period of about a decade. Initially prone to violent outbursts of rage, suicidality, amnesia, and infantile regression, within months she had developed a profound transference characterized by intense dependency and an idealized wish to be rescued. Though quite challenging and intimidating, she eventually became more manageable, responsible, and rather likeable. During a stay in the fifth year of treatment, after a series of humiliating enactments on the unit and after revealing a devastating secret, she staggered into my office, plopped on the couch, and started mumbling incoherently. I thought I heard her say something about taking a bottle of pills and noticed a bottle in her jacket pocket. It was empty. She had gone on a short pass to get personal supplies from the drugstore prior to her appointment. To my sudden horror, I realized she had a suicide plan which was coming to fruition right before my eyes. She stopped talking and lapsed into an obtunded state. Saliva dribbled out of the corner of her mouth. I called 911.

In the minutes it took for the fire rescue squad to arrive and fill my office with EMTs and police, I was absolutely stunned. Time seemed to stand still. I wondered if she would die on the couch before they arrived. She had been absolutely furious with me and then got eerily calm the day before. I wondered if I would find myself performing CPR and mouth-to-mouth resuscitation to try to keep her alive. It would have been an ironic "boundary violation" in light of her recent revelation. I felt the extraordinary, controlling power of her rage and projective identification as she, the ultimate victim, sought revenge against me through suicide. Now I, too, was angry, very frightened, and felt like a victim.

Had she not been rushed to the ER and expertly treated in the ICU, she undoubtedly would have died. Her drug level was off the charts and her doctors were rather pessimistic about her survival until the level had normalized rather quickly and uneventfully. To put it bluntly, she was "damn lucky." I visited her daily and felt my anger rise as her drug level dropped, realizing more and more how I had become an unwitting participant in her sexual exploitation and near fatal suicidal reaction. Now she was a captive audience in the ICU and I had to temper my feelings lest my "interpretations" become my own form of revenge in the form of blunt blows to her paper-thin psyche. I wanted to yell, how could you have done this *to me?*! Don't you understand who I really am??? Interestingly, I felt so personally attacked, hurt, unappreciated, and misunderstood that even with her in the ICU attached to monitors, oxygen, and IV lines, I was aware of how little empathy I felt at the time. I could not and did not want to hide my anger, so when Mrs. V awoke enough to recognize me and have some grasp of the gravity of the situation we began to talk about it. She was utterly surprised to still be alive, felt terrible shame and remorse for what she had done, and then sobbed uncontrollably. She feared that I could never trust her again, would refuse to treat her anymore, and would never speak to her again. She could read my thoughts clearly from my grave expression which I quietly confirmed, but I also added that there was an alternative scenario I could envision.

I told her that if she did pull through, that if she could tolerate hearing, feeling, and understanding the impact all of this had had upon *me*, analyze all we knew about what led up to it, and if she truly promised she would never try to take her life again and genuinely mean it, then we could continue. If she were in agreement, then the "only" thing she had to do was stay alive and, for the time being, just let her body recover and not worry about losing me. She seemed enormously relieved and continued to sob for what felt like a lifetime of loss and grief. This interchange was momentous as she, for the first time, began to think that things could be different. As such, it had the quality of a "now moment" (Stern et al., 1998). I, too, felt somewhat relieved, believing that she was capable of living up to her end of the deal but knowing that very painful and uncertain times lay ahead. In due course, she was medically stabilized and transferred back to the psychiatric institution where we continued to meet five times a week and explored her failed suicide in great detail. For the sake of brevity, I will summarize what we reconstructed.

Just prior to her OD, Mrs. V became enraged with me when she believed that I was favoring another patient over her. She felt intensely competitive with and jealous of this woman with whom she had become quite friendly. Mrs. V thought that I spent more time with her rival, liked her more and, more important, always believed her side of the story when it pertained to strife on the unit involving these two rather visible members of the in-patient community. As a result, she suddenly felt very unsafe and very alone in a mental hospital in a distant city far from home. This triangular enactment was especially charged because she was just beginning to let her last and most dangerous secret be revealed—that something sexual might be happening between her and her local therapist.

As such, this smaller enactment was nested within a much larger, ongoing secret enactment. Being an adult survivor of severe childhood physical and sexual abuse, much of her history had already been reconstructed through integrating her verbalization, artwork, journaling, dreams, dreamlike altered states of consciousness, and the analysis of repetitive enactments which usually centered around personal boundaries or testing the consistency of limits on the unit. For example, she would secretly triumph over not getting caught smoking in her room but would scream in outrage and destroy property when she felt falsely accused of the slightest infraction. At times in the past, her violent outbursts toward staff required her being put in restraints and receiving intramuscular medication. Years later when we could comfortably reminisce about these "bad old days," Mrs. V recalled with horror and just a bit of mischievous glee the time she broke out of her restraints like "Hercules unchained." She felt a sense of omnipotence as the staff was taken aback and unprepared for her sudden burst of strength and fury. In order to accomplish this last-resort form of behavioral control, several staff were needed to subdue this rather strong woman, but in the process would invariably participate in a sadomasochistic enactment of a gang rape.

During one particularly chaotic hospitalization, she went AWOL in an amnesic rage, went to a local hotel where she picked up a man, had violent sex with him, and then went into an absolute panic when she "came to" in a childlike state and did not know where she was. When a more compliant adult self reconstituted, she called the unit but was terrified to reveal her whereabouts lest we call the police and have her arrested for prostitution. Her guilt was enormous and of lethal proportion. As though she were negotiating a hostage situation over her dissociated selves, the patient insisted that I be called and would only negotiate with me. A part of her, I later learned, had wanted me to come to the hotel and pick her up personally but her erotic transference wish would have then been too obvious and laden with intolerable guilt, so she regressed to a naïve, asexual childlike state looking to be saved. I sensed her abject fear and became aware of my own fantasy to do just that. I heard in her infantile crying a pathetic, unheeded plea for some good person somewhere—finally—to rescue her from the dangerous man she was so adept at re-finding in her life.

Her stepfather raped both her and her mother at will but preferred his young stepdaughter and eventually ignored his wife who, in turn, turned a blind eye. A most disturbing memory of that time which had emerged was of the family watching TV together at night. The scene consisted of the patient sitting on her stepfather's lap with no underwear while he quietly penetrated her as the mother, absorbed in the TV show, sat across the darkened room oblivious to the incest. Furthermore, the stepfather was known for his cruelty and domination of others; he especially liked to destroy young Mrs. V's soul (Shengold, 1989) by inducing her to want sex with him by depriving her of food and other necessities and then rewarding her for her compliance and secrecy. She was given ice cream and money for being "a special girl." She learned at an early age to keep such secrets, which is exactly what she had done with regard to her local therapist's sexual demands. In her experience, no one would listen, care, or believe her. Even if they did, they would not dare to confront her brutal stepfather, so she did not expect to be believed and helped here either.

Mrs. V had had several very serious suicide attempts in the past and after the realization that her childhood incestuous relationship had evolved into a more overtly mutual affair which persisted well into her married, adult years, she desperately wanted to kill herself again. This history was first enacted in a dissociated state after she belatedly confessed that upon her discharge from the hospital one time she met a former male patient she had befriended and had intercourse with him in a hotel. This pattern of furtive sexual behavior seemed to recreate the stepfather's incest in the presence of the mother who was unwilling and unable to know about it and protect her daughter. In this case, it was happening under my nose and she was perversely thrilled and mortified by getting away with it.

Recognizing the pattern enabled us to also see the underlying maternal transference she so deeply projected onto me. Mrs. V's disappointment and rage at her mother were limitless, and in a series of macabre, virtual family sessions with her mother's ashes stored in Tupperware and FedEx'ed to her for the occasion, she expressed her bitterness and sorrow in a most eerie but effective way. These abreactions with her mother's cremated remains facilitated her complicated mourning process, which was replete with anniversary reactions and suicidal despair as the annual date of her mother's death occurred. So, when one of her dissociated child selves emerged in the session to reveal that her local therapist was currently doing things to her like her daddy used to, the familiar paradigm was immediately clear. This time, however, her reward for compliance and secrecy was getting his help in making arrangements with her insurance company for her to come back to the hospital to continue working with me. His sadistic manipulation of this most vulnerable patient for his sexual pleasure used coming to see me as her reward and made it impossible in her transference longings to experience me as a safe, protective mother for any sustained period of time.

I became her ice cream cone laced with psychological poison. All of these factors conspired to create the clinical "perfect storm" which culminated in her wish to kill herself and die in my arms on my couch. She had totally given up hope as she felt betrayed by her mother once again in the transference.

DISCUSSION

The sexual relationship with her local therapist had developed slowly over a period of years and, in her naïve and susceptible state, she felt special, loved, and very important to him. This therapist evidently knew this about her, having learned of her most vulnerable child "selves." These were actually psychological structures that served many functions, including encapsulation of the patient's memories and self and object representations associated with early sadomasochistic sexual abuse by the stepfather. Instead of allowing these defensive altered states to emerge spontaneously in the context of analytically oriented therapy or accessing them through hypnosis as part of a rational structured treatment plan known as the tactical integrationalist approach (Fine, 1993; Kluft, 1993), he apparently would summon a certain little girl self named Honey because he knew she would be sexually compliant and keep the secret. In fact, she was a clinical "sitting duck" (Kluft, 1990). She described with deep mortification how it happened the first time. One day he nonchalantly commented on the shape of her body and asked her what brand of lingerie she wore since his wife was also shaped that way and had trouble finding comfortable undergarments. Mrs. V innocently said she did not know what brand she had and when asked if he could come behind her and check the labels, she "didn't think anything about it" and said okay. Then her mind went blank and she had amnesia for the rest of the session but was left with sexual sensations and a queasy feeling in her stomach when she "came to" after the session. Through artwork and eventually words, Mrs. V in her child state tearfully described his tender, seductive words in her ear, calling for Honey, his "special girl," his removal of her bra, touching of her breasts, and the sounds of his heavy breathing and noises consistent with masturbation. From events like this, the patient in various states of mind recounted a series of unacknowledged sexual experiences progressing to intercourse. When she learned that he was under some type of investigation, she was initially dumbfounded.

Devastation, jealousy, and rage came much later. In fact, she was in such a state of dissociated denial that when the therapist had the temerity to ask her for a letter of reference attesting to his good character, she was inclined to do so! When she asked my opinion about a year before her own experiences came to light, I asked her directly if she had any reason to question his professionalism. She convincingly told me that she trusted him and that the only doubt she had was pertaining to his asking her some business advice about which she was knowledgeable in order to help him with his own side business. At the time I found the story a bit disconcerting and was reminded of the fact that the very few times I had spoken with him over the phone he seemed either brusque, disinterested, or so totally knowledgeable about his patient's condition that he was doing me a favor. At the time, Mrs. V's emphatic denial of any deeper problems with him was such that any further inquiry on my part would undoubtedly have been experienced as a mean interrogation by a disbelieving authority figure and have damaged our alliance. Subsequently, when she later was informed that a number of very angry patients had filed complaints against him, she became very shaken up and agitated.

Doubts, recurrent dreams, auditory hallucinations, and somatic sensations began to emerge which made her wonder if she, too, had been victimized in her autohypnotic states, but she had blocked it out of her mind. At such times, the patient would become very estranged from her usual self (Putnam, 1989), lapsing into a state of knowing and not knowing, being there and not being there, and feeling that it was her and not her. Exploiting her desperate need to be accepted, loved, and thought well of, she had become aware through our work that at times she felt she had no choice but to comply as a result of her inability to know herself or be except through another's reality and the demands made upon her (Whitmer, 2001). Her profound fears of rejection and abandonment betrayed a disturbance in both object and self-constancy as submission to even a perpetrator was preferable to being alone, as it staved off annihilation anxiety, and a reaction to object loss which resembled the disorganized attachment behavior of a disturbed infant.

As a two-person model of defense and conflict, such early attachment behaviors form the basis of the "unthought known" (Bollas, 1987), i.e., implicit enactive memories which predate the development of symbolization and explicit memory (Stern et al., 1998; Lyons-Ruth, 1999). As such, there is mounting evidence of a pathodevelopmental line from disorganized infant attachment to "internalized dialogue as defense" to dissociative phenomena. There is considerable research to support Main and Hesse's (1990) hypothesis that unresolved fear in the parent is transmitted through behavior which conveys that fear or other behavior which frightens the infant (Jacobovitz, Hazen, and Riggs, 1997; Lyons-Ruth, Bronfman, and Parsons, 1999; Schwengel, Bakermans-Kronenberg, and Van Ijzendoorn, 1999). What was known of Mrs. V's mother suggests that she, too, was traumatized, lived in fear, and may also have had a dissociative disorder.

These findings suggest that the clinical treatment which fosters collaboration and healthy dialogue would facilitate an integrated experience for the patient. This idea is not unlike Bromberg's (1994), which sees dissociation as a ubiquitous, interpersonal defense because what is not known is not unconscious intrapsychically but unthinkable because it was not properly recognized by the primary caretaker. Whitmer (2001), however, goes on to define the defensive aspects of dissociation as ultimately an intrapsychic inhibition of finding meaning in experience in that it is an active decoupling of a biologically prepared process as described by Fonagy (1991). It therefore follows that in families where abuse occurs, a climate of denial of it exists and that absence of acknowledgment in the caretaker/child dyad promotes a dissociative state of mind.

Such a disturbance as seen in Mrs. V, according to Stern's (1985) model, would infer problems in the very early development of the core self, especially in the areas of self-cohesion, self-continuity, and self-agency. As such, dissociation is then seen as the quintessential example of the interpersonal nature of the self which must be defined in relation to the object. This plight has been defiantly proclaimed in the genre of rap music by the controversial superstar Eminem, in his song "The Way I Am." Such dependency on the mother's reality, if it persists into adulthood, results in a major impairment of the capacity to mentalize (Fonagy and Target, 1996). It also creates a paradox in that this very inability to think independently may leave the individual quite capable at times of becoming impervious to the influence of others.

This "illusion of an autonomous psyche" (Whitmer, 2001, p. 817), I would contend, is further enhanced, reconfigured, and carried to the extreme in cases of DID where there are seemingly separate selves or personifications which may deny or not know the existence of others. This phenomenon creates the illusion of cohesion of the self also, even though the different selves may be engaged in lethal, i.e., suicidal, battles over exclusive control of the body (Brenner, 2001, 2004). Not only would there be disturbances in the core self but also in the intersubjective self and quite dramatically in the narrative self (Stern, 1985) where the various dissociated personalities could claim to have different biographies. The vulnerability to submission and sadomasochistic exploitation is often seen in the scared child selves who cannot say "no" but who also reflect an exceedingly complex, intrapsychic structure which functions as a compromise formation (Brenner, 1982).

This duality of interpersonal and intrapsychic was poignantly illustrated to me when I realized that Mrs. V was reexperiencing on the couch and verbalizing with me what was being enacted in amnesic altered states with her psychotherapist when she went back home. Having achieved enough trust of me and preferring to avoid eye contact during sessions which intensified her feelings of shame, she often opted to use the couch for our sessions. By that time I had become quite familiar with her patterns of "switching" and could recognize these changes by the fluctuations in her voice, different use of language, predominant mental preoccupations, and gestures. Therefore, I did not need to rely on the changes in her facial expression or eyes, such as glazing over and eyelid fluttering, which often signal such an autohypnotic shift in mental state which is more easily recognizable by these latter cues.

I had also established a therapeutic alliance with most of her personifications so that if I were unsure I could ask and be generally assured of getting a reliable response. As a result, the mosaic of dissociated conversations revealed that she frequently experienced uncontrollable sexual arousal associated with memories of her stepfather and feelings in the transference. When not warded off by switching to an asexual child self or an angry, threatening self, she would lapse into states of autoerotic pleasure of orgasmic proportion. At such times she confessed with much hesitation that she felt so much longing and vulnerability that she would not be able to say "no" to me or anyone else who might make sexual overtures to her. During these times, her intrapsychic conflict over her wishes was quite evident but in an unusual form. Although fear, guilt, and self-destructive urges were deeply felt, Mrs. V employed a particular defense which I have described as pseudo-externalized displacement. Aggression and sexual longings were disowned, banished from consciousness, and attributed to someone else—in this case, that someone else was not an outside person but rather an "inside" self (Brenner, 2001). Working with this defense as it emerged in the transference was a crucial part of the treatment as it involved her altered states, amnesia, traumatic memories, and pathognomic development of her dissociated selves.

CONCLUSION

In conclusion, such patients with early trauma, severe dissociative psychopathology, and aberrant development of the self are extremely enactment-prone and susceptible to sadomasochistic, exploitative relationships. They may feel inexorably drawn to those who recreate early disturbed attachment and perpetrator relatedness, feeling unable to resist and assert a sense of self-agency. Such "fatal attractions" may, indeed, become just that. In this case, Mrs. V could only extricate herself from her therapist with much outside help. Her "brainwashing" (Shengold, 1989) from childhood required her to keep the secret of her sexual relationship with him as she felt both terrorized and specially loved. Addressing such vulnerabilities in treatment requires attending to both the interactive precursors as well as the intrapsychic manifestations of dissociation.

REFERENCES

Bollas, C. (1987). *The Shadow of the Object: Psychoanalysis of the Unthought Unknown*. New York: Columbia University Press.

Bowlby, J. (1969). *Attachment and Loss: Vol. Attachment*. New York: Basic.

Brenner, C. (1982). *The Mind in Conflict*. New York: International University Press.

Brenner, I. (2001). *Dissociation of Trauma: Theory, Phenomenology and Technique*. Madison, CT: International University Press.

———. (2004). *Psychic Trauma: Dynamics, Symptoms, and Treatment*. Lanham, MD: Jason Aronson.

Bromberg, P. (1994). "Speak! that I may see you": Some reflections on dissociation, reality, and psychoanalytic listening. *Psychoanalytic Dialogues*, 4:517–547.

Ferenczi, S. (1932). Diary entries: January 19, June 3, July 21, 1932. *The Clinical Diary of Sandor Ferenczi*, ed. J. Dupont, transl. M. Balint and N. Z. Jackson, pp. 13–16, 115, 162–166. Cambridge, MA: Harvard University Press, 1988.

Fine, C. (1993). A tactical integrationalist perspective on the treatment of multiple personality disorder. In *Clinical Perspectives on Multiple Personality Disorder*, eds. R. P. Kluft and C. G. Fine, pp. 135–153. Washington, DC: American Psychiatric Press.

Fonagy, P. (1991). Thinking about thinking: Some clinical and theoretical considerations. *International Journal of Psychoanalysis* 72:1–18.

———, and Target, M. (1996). Playing with reality: Theory of mind and the normal development of psychic reality. *International Journal of Psychoanalysis* 77:217–233.

Freud, S. (1905). A fragment of an analysis of a case of hysteria. S.E. VII, p. 109.

———. (1912). Recommendations to physicians practicing psychoanalysis. S.E. XII.

Gabbard, G., and Lester, E. (1995). *Boundaries and Boundary Violations in Psychoanalysis*. New York: Basic.

Jacobovitz, D., Hazen, N., and Riggs, S. (1997). Disorganized mental processes in mothers, frightening/frightened caregiving and disoriented/disorganized behavior in infancy. Paper presented at symposium, Caregiving Correlates and Longitudinal Outcomes of Disorganized Attachments in Infants, Biennial Meeting of the Society for Research in Child Development. Washington, DC.

Kales, E. F. (2003). Fatal attraction. *International Journal of Psychoanalysis* 84:1631–1637.

Kluft, R. P. (1990). Incest and subsequent revictimization: The case of therapist-patient exploitation, with a description of the sitting duck syndrome. In *Incest Re-*

lated Syndromes of Adult Psychopathology, ed. R. P. Kluft, pp. 263–287. Washington, DC: American Psychiatric Press.

———. (1993). Clinical approaches to the integration of personalities. In *Clinical Perspectives on Multiple Personality Disorder*, eds. R. P. Kluft and C. G. Fine, pp. 101–134. Washington, DC: American Psychiatric Press.

Lyons-Ruth, K. (1999). The two-person unconscious: Intersubjective dialogue, enactive relational representation and the emergence of new forms of relational organization. *Psychoanalytic Inquiry* 19:576–617.

———, Alpern, L., and Repacholi, B. (1993). Disorganized infant attachment classification and maternal psychosocial problems as predictors of hostile-aggressive behavior in the preschool classroom. *Child Development* 64:572–585.

Lyons-Ruth, K., Bronfman, E., and Parsons, E. (1999). Maternal disrupted affective communication, maternal frightened or frightening behavior, and disorganized infant attachment strategies. In *Atypical Patterns of Infant Attachment: Theory, Research, and Current Directions*, eds. J. Vondra and D. Barnett, *Monographs of the Society for Research in Child Development* (Serial No. 258), pp. 67–96.

Mahler, M., Bergman, A., and Pine, F. (1975). *The Psychological Birth of the Human Infant*. New York: Basic Books.

Main, M., and Hesse, E. (1990). Parents' unresolved traumatic experiences are related to infant disorganized status: Is parental frightened or frightening behavior in the linking mechanism? In *Attachment in the Preschool Years: Theory, Research, and Intervention*, eds. M. Greenberg, D. Cicchetti, and E. M. Cummings, pp. 161–184. Chicago: University of Chicago Press.

Main, M., and Solomon, J. (1990). Procedures for identifying infants as disorganized/disoriented during the Ainsworth Strange Situation. In *Attachment in the Preschool Years: Theory, Research, and Intervention*, eds. M. Greenberg, D. Cicchetti, and E. M. Cummings, pp. 121–160. Chicago: University of Chicago Press.

Putnam, F. (1989). *Diagnosis and Treatment of Multiple Personality Disorder*. New York: Guilford Press.

Schwengel, C., Bakermans-Kronenberg, M., and Van Ijzendoorn, M. (1999). Frightening maternal behavior linking unresolved loss and disorganized infant attachment. *Journal of Consulting and Clinical Psychology* 67:54–63.

Shengold, L. (1989). *Soul Murder: The Effects of Child Abuse and Deprivation*. New Haven, CT: Yale University Press.

Stern, D. (1985). *The Interpersonal World of the Infant*. New York: International University Press.

———, Sander, L., Nahum, J., Harrison, A., Lyons-Ruth, K., Morgan, A., Bruschweiler-Stern, N., and Tronick, E. Z. (1998). Noninterpretive mechanisms in psychoanalytic therapy. *International Journal Psychoanalysis* 79: 903–921.

Whitmer, G. (2001). On the nature of dissociation. *Psychoanalysis Quarterly* 70:807–837.

6

Breaking of Boundaries and Craving for Oneness

Ilany Kogan, M.A.

In this chapter I wish to explore the breaking of internal and external boundaries as a result of trauma, viewed from cultural, developmental, and clinical perspectives. This will be illustrated with a case study of a patient who was the son of Holocaust survivor parents. The patient's mother, who became ill after his birth, committed suicide at the age of 54, and the patient's son took his own life at age 20, when the patient was in his second year of analytic treatment. I will focus on the cultural perspective—the impact of the traumatic Holocaust past of the parents on the patient's outer interpersonal boundaries and on their internalized dimensions. This will include the developmental aspect of the patient's relationship with his parents who were emotionally and physically damaged by their traumatic Holocaust past to the extent that they allowed outer interpersonal boundaries between generations to be destroyed by an incestuous relationship between mother and son. I will demonstrate the impact of the perverse physical and emotional closeness with the mother on the son's cognitive and emotional development and on his psychic structure.

This will be followed by an analysis of the patient's fantasies and enactments, demonstrating how the mother's violent past intruded into the patient's present and broke boundaries between past and present, fantasy and reality, and self and object. In addition, the interplay between present trauma (the son's suicide) and the memory of past trauma (the mother's suicide) and its impact on the patient will be explored.

I will also examine the impact of trauma on the breaking of boundaries from the clinical perspective, and discuss the approach I used in treating this patient. The clinical perspective will deal with the patient's breaking of the analytic boundaries of time, place, and abstinence from touch. These boundaries, which represent the reality principle (Freud, 1911) and are "the guardians of separateness and of the incest barrier at a deeper, unconscious level" (Akhtar, 1999, p. 116), may be regarded by the analyst as an extension of his own outer ego boundaries (Epstein, 1994). I will illustrate how the patient used the breaking of analytic boundaries to actualize his craving for oneness with the analyst in his attempt to repeat the incestuous relationship with his mother. I will describe the effect of his breaking of boundaries on the analyst, the impact of the son's suicide on the treatment, and how the analyst dealt with this very difficult situation.

CASE ILLUSTRATION

The First Encounter

David, a 54-year-old engineer, married for the second time and father of three, sought professional help for exhaustion, depression, difficulty functioning at work, and thoughts of suicide. He suffered from various somatic conditions like high blood pressure, chronic fatigue, psoriasis, and sexual impotence. He was extremely frustrated with his situation at work and felt that life was not worth living. He occasionally entertained thoughts of jumping off a tall building and ending his suffering.

David was born after World War II to parents who had been physically and emotionally damaged by the Holocaust. David's father left his parents' home in Transylvania and immigrated to Budapest before the war. His father's family—his parents, all of his brothers and sisters, with the exception of one sibling who had escaped to the United States—were killed in the Holocaust. When war broke out, the couple, being very poor, sought refuge in "Wallenberg's Houses," an area protected by the Swedish embassy. The mother's family, who lived in the more affluent section of the city, was taken to a concentration camp and never returned. The young couple survived.

David was born under unusual circumstances. He was told that his mother, like so many other women during the Holocaust, had been given injections of hormones to stop her menstrual cycle and prevent conception. When the war ended, David's father took her to Romania, where she received other injections to restore her fertility. In spite of the doctors' pessimistic prognosis, she became pregnant with David. The doctors regarded

David's birth as a miracle. After his birth, David's mother became very ill. She later developed cancer, possibly from the initial hormonal treatment, and her health deteriorated greatly. At the age of 54 she committed suicide, following an operation to remove the cancerous growth.

After David's birth, his father learned of the death of his parents and siblings in a concentration camp, and he became depressed and emotionally withdrawn. Thus, David the "miracle child" grew up with a physically ill mother and an emotionally absent father.

The family remained in Romania until after David's birth and then returned to Hungary, where both parents found work. In 1957, with the Russian suppression of the revolution against the communist regime, the entire area where they lived, including their house, was bombed. As a result of the bombing, David, then 10 years old, suffered a nervous breakdown and had to be hospitalized. He remembered the separation from his mother as the most traumatic element of his hospitalization.

The relationship between David and his mother was a special one. At the end of our initial interview, during which David recounted the story of his life, he said: "There is something I haven't yet told you. It is the biggest secret of my life. I have one last wish—to sleep with my mother!" Seeing the amazed expression on my face, he added: "In her grave." The pleasure David derived from my shock and amazement indicated the perverse nature of the transference relationship from the very start, and was predictive of further encounters of this sort.

David saw his mother as the anchor of his life, giving him the strength to overcome its hardships and persevere. She was the dominant figure at home, and had a derogatory attitude toward his father, whom David experienced as weak and irrelevant to the family. The father, the weak, castrated figure at home, became a devoted communist who fought for the welfare of the poor. David knew that his father had been involved in extramarital relationships.

David was a problematic child who developed slowly. For several years, the doctors thought him mentally retarded. He was fat, clumsy, and often rejected by other children. He suffered from enuresis nocturna until the age of 14. David was very close to his mother, and he slept in bed with her until he was around 17 years old.

David's first sexual encounter was with an older woman, a friend of the family who at the time was his father's lover. He claimed that his mother knew about his relationship with the woman but never interfered.

Talking about his family life, David described two unsuccessful attempts to escape from Hungary. The first occurred when he finished high school and became a waiter on a train that crisscrossed the country, placing a geographical distance between his mother and himself. He liked the job, but his mother asked him to give it up and come back home. The second attempt took place after several years of marriage and two children. His wife was a non-Jewish, Hungarian woman from a primitive family. He had married her because she was tall and stout, physically resembling his mother. After several years of marriage, he was no longer in love with her and resolved to leave his family. He went to a football match in the West and decided to remain there. Again, it was his mother who demanded that he return home, and he obediently complied.

At the age of 54, the mother underwent an operation for a cancerous growth in her stomach. The doctors informed the family that the operation had been successful and that she would soon recover, but a few days later she was found dead in her hospital bed. The rumor was that she had committed suicide. David felt that he had missed the opportunity to take leave of his mother. He felt that her death was the loss of his protective shield, leaving him vulnerable and helpless, like a child. Several months after her death, David felt there was no longer anything to keep him in Hungary. He arranged a trip to Germany and, without bidding farewell to his wife and children, went abroad and never returned.

From Germany David immigrated to Israel, where he attempted to embark upon a new life. He soon developed a relationship with a prosperous, well-educated woman. Like the wife he had abandoned, she too bore a physical resemblance to his mother. David divorced his wife and married her. He decided that it would be best for him to make a total break with his former family; by not having any contact with them, he erased them from his life.

David claimed that his new wife abhorred the idea of having children, and as long as they had none they were happy together. But after several years, she changed her mind and even underwent fertility treatment to become pregnant. Finally she gave birth to a son, Avi. The relationship, which David had described as idyllic, changed completely, their togetherness destroyed by the birth of the child. David described his wife as a demanding, coercive mother who was incapable of giving their son the boundless love he had received from his own mother. Her obsession with order and cleanliness was a constant source of conflict. She had frequent outbursts of anger, and would shout furiously at him as well as at the child.

From a very early age, their son had difficulty accepting authority, and David's wife accused David of being incapable of disciplining him. David felt he was playing the maternal role in the relationship with his son, by fulfilling the child's every whim, unable to set any limits. The child was an underachiever in school and a loner. He developed into an angry, schizoid adolescent, who would close himself up in his room for hours and barely speak to his parents. He developed a passion for chess, and spent endless hours playing chess by himself in his room. David was very worried about him. He claimed that the boy was very much like himself, only more so.

During the Gulf War, while serving in the army reserve, David volunteered for a special unit that would rush to the place where a scud had landed to see whether chemical warfare was involved. David was always among the first to arrive on the scene, omnipotently believing that he would survive even if the bomb had a chemical warhead.

Following in his father's footsteps, his son volunteered for the same army division, which now served in a dangerous area in the Gaza Strip. He was a problematic soldier and had great difficulty accepting authority. He was often in conflict with his officers and had been imprisoned several times for disobeying orders. David was aware that his son was exposed to danger, and expressed great concern for his life.

Phase I: Breaking Analytic Boundaries—the Incestuous Touch

In the first phase of analysis I became aware of David's concrete way of thinking. David spent much time ruminating over his unhappiness, attributing it mainly to his failure to obtain a managerial position in his company. Elaborating upon the unconscious meaning of his frustrated wishes and expectations over becoming a manager at work, I pointed out to David the great difficulty he had managing (having control over) his own body, as evidenced by the many illnesses he had suffered from. This interpretation facilitated elaboration of his wish to control that which was so important to him. In this regard, David revealed another secret—that he liked to watch sadomasochistic movies, enjoying the sight of brutal men tying up, beating, and sexually abusing women. David believed that his current impotence was a result of masturbating while watching these movies. He was addicted, watching the movies at home when alone, or in his office, instead of working. He was turned on mainly by the women who, in spite of being big and strong, were willing to do everything to please their torturers. In the transference, I soon realized that I had become the focus of David's masturbatory fantasies. I was the big, strong woman whom he wanted to torture to achieve sexual gratification.

As analysis continued, I began to experience David as a torturer. I will present some examples of his behavior that expressed his unconscious aggression toward me. Upon entering my office, David usually paused at the door and, unlike my other patients, waited for me to go in first, following me from behind. This gave me an uneasy feeling that he might attack me unawares. At the end of a session, David would again pause at the door of my office, looking me over with appreciative glances. David rejected all of my efforts to understand this unusual form of behavior, claiming that he was simply behaving like a gentleman. On a nonverbal level, I felt invaded by the smell of his very strong aftershave, which always made me open the window of my office after he left. I felt that David was trying to intrude into my privacy, my home, my body. I often tried to make him aware of the aggression beneath his behavior, but in vain. "Aggression toward you?" he would ask in amazement. "How can you say that; you know how I feel about you!" But in fact, I felt I knew much more about it than he did.

An incident that occurred during this period in analysis greatly increased my awareness of his unconscious, destructive wishes. At the end of a session, David got up from the couch and patted me lightly on the shoulder. I was dumbfounded, feeling that he had intruded upon my "perimeter of safety" (McLaughlin, 1995). David left and I, shocked by his breaking the taboo, tried to sort out my feelings. It gradually dawned upon me that David's enactment was probably a repetition of the forbidden touching which took place while in bed with his mother until late adolescence.

David's powerful aggression, which was directed against me, made me feel helpless and impotent. Could I function as an analyst when confronted with the destruction of boundaries inherent in his perverse behavior? Was it at all possible for me to work with this patient, and was analysis the treatment of choice for him? I began entertaining great doubts that it was.

Gradually, I realized that David regarded me as a figure that embodied both mother/therapist and prostitute. Moreover, I was an incestuous mother, who sexually abused her children. An episode in the transference illustrates this: Upon hearing the doorbell ring when the next patient arrived a few minutes early, he said, "This is not an analytic couch, this is a warm bed!" And he immediately added, "I know you have many patients, I am not your one and only." Thus, I was a prostitute who had many clients as well as a mother whose children lay on her couch one after the other.

Only later in analysis could we realize how vital it was for David to be my "one and only." The acting out that followed the above episode revealed more of David's anger and potential destructiveness. Driving back home after the session, a taxi suddenly obstructed David's way, forcing him to stop. Despite the heavy traffic behind him, he got out of his car and began shouting at and cursing the stunned taxi driver. David told me that he would have killed the taxi driver that very moment had he had a weapon on him. He was tormented by this incident and felt threatened by his uncontrollable aggression.

In the transference relationship we tried to understand who the man was who had evoked so much anger and aggression in him. Was it possible that I was the taxi driver here in analysis, and he experienced me as obstructing his way? Or perhaps his rage was evoked by the patient who had rung the doorbell at the end of the last session, the person who made him feel that he was not receiving my undivided attention. Did David want to kill all my "sons" so that he could remain my "one and only"?

David then proceeded to tell me about an episode of acting out during his vacation which had tormented him greatly. He had traveled from Paris to Hungary, his country of origin, to attend a conference. In Budapest he came across a lady who had been a close friend of his parents. The lady shared some personal details of her current life with David, telling him how very concerned she was about her son's life and career and her hurt over his alienated behavior. David advised her to erase the son from her life, to forget him as he had forgotten his sons from his previous family.

During this encounter, in which David shared some personal details about his own life, he suddenly found himself making love to the lady. David emphasized that he had never before cheated on his wife, and was therefore puzzled by his own behavior. In the transference I told David that this episode might have been an enactment of his sexual wishes toward me, evoked by the emotional closeness he experiences with me in analysis. David had no qualms accepting my interpretation.

At this stage of analysis (after a period of one year), David informed me of his desire to stop treatment for financial reasons. My attempt to inquire into the libidinal and aggressive motives behind this unexpected decision was a total failure. Unsuccessful in preventing David from leaving treatment, I told him that I respected his decision to leave although I did not agree with it, and that I would be here for him should he change his mind. David expressed his gratitude, stressing that he would come back to analysis as soon as he could.

Phase II: Breaking Analytic Boundaries of Time and Place

David never realized his wish to leave analysis. The traumatic event that occurred that same week changed his mind. I shall describe it in detail: At nine o'clock in the evening I received a phone call from David saying that he was canceling his sessions for all of next week. In answer to my enquiry about what happened, he replied in a tone devoid of emotion, "My son committed suicide." "What?" I said, shocked and horrified. "I was afraid this would happen," he answered. "I am not surprised; I will come to my session next week after the *shiva* is over." (*Shiva*, meaning "seven," is the Jewish mourning period, in which the bereaved remain at home for seven days, usually sitting together in the house of the deceased. During this week, friends and family visit and offer their condolences, share memories, and thus provide emotional support.)

Unfortunately, the following week a tragic event occurred in my own life. My father, aged 96, died after a prolonged illness. I phoned all my patients, telling them that I would be away for the following week for personal reasons. One can imagine my amazement when, during the week of *shiva* in my father's apartment in another city, I opened the door to find David standing there. He was wearing a black skullcap on his head and a beard adorned his face. (It is a Jewish custom that a man does not shave during the first month of mourning. Wearing a *kippa* [skullcap] is a sign of respect to God that is common during mourning, even among non-religious Jews.) He came in and sat down with an ease that was in stark contrast to my discomfort at seeing him. David said, "I saw the announcement in the newspaper and decided to visit you. So you are also in mourning, you are 'sitting *shiva*' like I did last week." (It is customary to put an advertisement in the newspaper, including the name of the deceased and the name of the family in mourning. Traditionally, the house of the deceased is open to visitors and paying a visit to the bereaved is considered a "good deed" [*mitzvah*].)

Confronted by David's breaking all boundaries, I felt totally helpless. David's condolence visit to me in my father's home destroyed the psychoanalytic setup, the borders of time and place, as well as the asymmetry existing between us. My embarrassment grew even greater when my son, aged 31, came into the room, gave me a kiss on the cheek, and said, "Hi, Mom, how are you?" David looked at him and said, "I am a patient of your mother's," and after several moments added, "My son committed suicide a week ago." I could see the amazement and confusion on my son's face. My son remained for a few minutes, made an excuse, and left. "There was no place for me there," he told me afterwards. David's visit lasted about 50 minutes. At the end of his visit he suddenly exclaimed, "I think that my son did what I wanted to do but didn't dare." In spite of my confusion and embarrassment, the complete breaking of analytic rules and the violent intrusion into my life, I was also aware of David's tremendous need to see me after his misfortune and of the fact that I was giving him an analytic session under very strange circumstances.

Working through my own feelings regarding this episode, I had to sort through some difficult questions: Why did David tell my son about the suicide, I wondered. Was he trying to erase my son from my life by implying— "Do the same, vanish from here!" so that David could remain my "one and only"? If he had unconsciously wished to erase his own son from his life, how was he coping now that his wish had been realized by the boy's self-destructive act? The elaboration of David's unconscious wishes and guilt feelings regarding his son's suicide was possible only later in analysis.

Phase III: The Manic Period—Denial, Omnipotence, and Sexual Promiscuity

The following week David resumed analysis, viewing his decision to stop treatment as no longer relevant. The beginning of this phase was characterized by David's manic defenses and euphoric demeanor, which enabled him to avoid pain. Thus, he was preoccupied with the important visitors who came to pay their condolences during the *shiva*, and also kept himself busy with the special prayers recited three times a day during the period of mourning.

After the first month of mourning was over, David began encountering enormous difficulty in accepting the reality of Avi's death. He felt it unlikely that his son had actually committed suicide, the futility of the act completely unacceptable to him. David raised the possibility that the death had been an accident, since Avi went around with a loaded gun, which was against army regulations. Unable to deal with his guilt, David offered many hypotheses for Avi's suicide. He projected the guilt upon Avi's officer and accused him of his son's self-destructive act. Apparently, the officer had threatened to put Avi in jail again for disobeying orders. David and his wife had wanted to write "murdered by his officer" on Avi's tombstone, but the military authorities refused. David also suggested that the suicide might actually have been an altruistic act, to publicly denounce the Israeli army's persecution of its own soldiers. Given this perspective, the self-destruction became an idealized act of strength and martyrdom.

In my countertransference, I felt how hard it was for David to deal with the pain and the narcissistic wound caused by Avi's suicide. At the same time, I found it difficult to witness David's mechanisms of self-deception and his efforts to avoid mourning at all cost. But knowing that, at this stage, these mechanisms were vital for his psychic survival, I was able to respect his defenses.

A major obstacle on the road to mourning was the eroticization of the transference and the sadomasochistic game that David began playing. I will illustrate this with the following example: David came into my office and, seeing my new lamp, began playing with the dimmer, making the room almost dark. The fear I had felt in the earlier stages of analysis began creeping up on me, as I again experienced David as potentially dangerous. In contrast to the earlier stages of analysis, however, I summoned my strength and spoke to David about his lack of respect for boundaries and his need for controlling the analytic situation. In this regard, I reminded him of his visit to my father's house during the *shiva*. The elaboration of this episode made David aware that he had indeed violated boundaries, but he did not find much wrong with it. He claimed that he, like Avi, had never adhered to rules, and that dealing with boundaries was extremely difficult for him. In this context, he recalled the absence of a father who could establish boundaries, and the presence of a mother who set no limits to the emotional and physical relationship between herself and her son, and who allowed him to sleep in her bed until the age of 17. David stated that he found the boundaries of the therapeutic relationship difficult. He mentioned that he had tried several times to get closer to me by asking me personal questions about myself, and he felt the wall I had erected between us. He longingly anticipated the analytic sessions, being with me in my office, our discussions. The time boundary, my sending him out in the cold at the end of 45 minutes, was simply unbearable. "What am I going to do with these feelings?" asked David. "I was like a train traveling toward death, and suddenly a locomotive came and led me in the other direction, toward life." We were quiet for a while and then he said, "You have many patients and I have only you."

In the following sessions David talked about his craving to be blissfully united with the woman he loved, which in the transference, was with me. Delving into his fantasies, we discovered that he wished to be with this woman in a kind of bubble, on a deserted island, with no one else around. He could not understand how he had had children from both marriages, as they interfered with the oneness with the woman he loved. In spite of this, his second wife even underwent artificial insemination to become pregnant. David explained that his sperm could not live in the acidic environment of a woman's body, and they therefore died in his wife's womb. If so, I said, perhaps he felt that he had almost died in his mother's womb. "Yes," answered David, "I did almost die there; I have already died many times." In the transference I pointed out to David that he was perhaps experiencing the analysis—my "womb"—as potentially dangerous for him because of my frequent attempts to put him in touch with his overwhelming feelings of pain and his mourning. Is it possible, I asked David, that he was trying to defend himself against what he felt was the "acidic" environment in analysis by infusing it with idealized qualities of warmth and intimacy, and was covering his pain and mourning with his erotic wishes? David reacted immediately to my questions: "There is a lot of pain in me and I am in mourning all the time. My son left a hole. It is impossible to fill it; there is a lot of death there inside me."

It gradually dawned upon me that whereas in the earlier stages of analysis I experienced David as my tormentor and myself as his victim, by putting David in touch with his feelings of mourning and guilt, I would become the sadistic, persecutory female (his internal maternal representation) that he expected me to be, which would make me a pawn in his sadomasochistic game. This realization was confirmed by David subsequently referring to me as being "my mythological mother, a Greek goddess!" To my question "What goddess?" "Medea," he answered without hesitance. "She killed her children, but what a woman! She slept with all the Gods!"

It was now clear to me that David was projecting his monstrous maternal representation upon me. On the one hand, David identified with the gods who enjoyed the sexual favors of this promiscuous mother; but, on the other hand, David was himself the battered child of a murderess mother, a child who was doomed to die at her own hand. Further psychic work was required for David to realize that he was identifying with this inner representation, and that at the same time that he was experiencing himself as her victim, he also felt he was a murderer. This was apparent from two consecutive dreams which David related during this period.

In the first dream, David saw Avi alive and coming back home from his army service. In the second dream, David and his father were attending a religious ceremony that included people of another religion, possibly Arabs. David's father was dressed as a priest. They brought in the head of a man in a golden glass bowl. The head was an offering to God. Everyone was praying to this head.

In his associations, David stated that the purpose of this offering was to unite with God. He recalled the biblical story of Abraham's readiness to sacrifice Isaac in order to fulfill God's wish. The story, in his view, showed how far Abraham was ready to go to achieve this union with God. The head in the golden bowl did not remind him of anyone he knew. His father, the priest, was presiding over the ceremony.

Was it possible, I wondered silently, that the head in the glass bowl was David's own head; that perhaps this was a decapitation (or, castration), in the presence of a father/priest, which David had inflicted upon himself as punishment for his incestuous cravings for oneness with a mother/goddess? Or, I continued to speculate, had David delegated death by decapitation to his son, Avi, who committed suicide in his stead, David thus committing suicide by proxy?

David raised another possibility in his further associations with regard to the offering to God in his dream: He again referred to the powerful, godlike wife/mother with whom he craved to be united in a blissful union, where he would be her "one and only." He would live with her in a kind of cocoon, without children and without worries. Following these associations, I pointed out to David the unconscious conflicting wishes battling inside him. His first dream expressed his wish to revivify his son and bring him back home. In his second dream, he decapitated his son in order to unite with a godlike figure. In this case, the head in the glass bowl was Avi's, and David perhaps felt that Avi had realized his father's wish to destroy him in order to achieve a blissful union with a godlike wife/mother. If this hypothesis was correct, I thought silently, then reality (Avi's suicide) had given credence to David's murderous fantasies, greatly increasing his feelings of omnipotence and "persecutory guilt" (Grinberg, 1964).

Attempting to escape pain and guilt, David's manic behavior continued. David was offered early retirement at work, which he happily accepted. Having lots of free time and enough money, he registered for an advanced course in his field, joined a fitness club, and worked on plans to establish a chess club in Avi's memory. He became an amusement freak, frequenting the theater, concerts, restaurants. In the midst of all this, he decided to check out his manhood in a "health club" located on the outskirts of the city; this was actually a whorehouse, where he received a "full massage" from a young girl. The outcome was a complete failure, but David stressed that "he paid the girl for her time, since she had worked hard on him."

This theme was repeated in another episode: David participated in an event arranged for bereaved families of soldiers who were killed during their army service, which took place in a hotel at the seashore. In his luxurious bedroom, David decided to check out the hotel's escort service. Using the Internet, he invited a girl to his room and she arrived promptly. He described the girl as being barely twenty years old, too young and too thin for his taste. He was unable to have full intercourse with her, but in spite of that, and maybe even because of it, he was sure that the girl had enjoyed it.

I was aware that in both erotic episodes described above, David mentioned that the whore was a young girl. It occurred to me that perhaps through these erotic encounters, David was enacting the trauma of his childhood. He, the older man, was playing the role of the mature parent who was sexually abusing the child, thus converting his infantile trauma into an adult triumph (Stoller, 1975).

I pointed out to David that he was placing me in the role of the whore with whom he wanted to have an erotic interchange. My transference interpretation had no emotional impact on him. David had no problem acknowledging his desire to have an affair with me; moreover, he talked about his physical relationship with his mother until late puberty as a source of pleasure. "Why shouldn't a son sleep in bed with his mother?" he asked with a smile. "It's forbidden only because of social conventions; otherwise, I don't see anything wrong with it." I felt helpless in front of his perverse structure and manic defenses. At the same time, I realized that it would be futile at this point to confront David with his negative feelings toward me, as he would totally reject them. I told David that he was apparently doing everything possible to avoid being in touch with his pain and bereavement. David confirmed this by saying, "Yes, I am just trying to get a good taste of life." Then he continued, "My son was only an episode in my life. I was here in this world before him and I'll be here after him." While this was an accurate statement, its monstrosity made me doubt not only my professional ability to help David work through his mourning, but also my emotional capacity to view him as human. I had to summon all my strength in order to remain "alive and whole" (Winnicott, 1971) and resume my therapeutic role.

Phase IV: From Manic Defense to Mourning—the Stabilization of Psychic Boundaries

The transition from manic defense to mourning began with David's wish to visit the place where Avi had committed suicide. It was extremely important for him to see where his son had spent the last moments of his life. Wishing to explore my notion that David felt he was a criminal, I said, "It seems to me as if you want to visit the scene of the crime." David took a deep breath and said, "Yes, that was the scene of the crime." Then he got up and said: "The question is—how did I contribute to that crime?"

In the period that followed, David's mood changed from mania to deep depression. He lost interest in sports, in his studies, and even gave up the plans for the chess club that he had wanted to establish in Avi's memory. He was unable to sleep through the night, and was extremely irritable and angry. At times he entertained fantasies of leaving his wife and going somewhere in the world where he could begin life anew; other times he expressed the wish to return to Hungary and take his own life, and thus, at long last, be blissfully united with his mother. I then asked David whether he wanted to leave me as well as analysis. David's spiteful answer confirmed my hypothesis: this treatment is sheer futility; he feels terribly tired, exhausted; I am not helping him; I never tell him what to do; all this delving into the past is totally useless; he needs some practical guidance. If it weren't for the fact that he wanted to be with me, he would have stopped the treatment ages ago.

This was the first time that David had attacked the treatment verbally. I reacted to David's irritated, bitter tone of voice, saying that I realized how angry he was at me for putting him in touch with his pain, and I stressed that by attacking the treatment he was trying to get rid of me. I added that he was now capable of expressing his anger toward me freely, which was a sign of progress.

Next session David informed me that he wanted to stop treatment. "I want a change, I want to throw away the crutches," he told me with a grin. In the countertransference, I felt the narcissistic hurt caused by being the "crutches," the inanimate object that David wished to discard. But, attempting to understand him brought several questions to mind: Was his behavior at this point an attempt to protect me from his own murderous rage and destructiveness? Was it possible that unconsciously he felt guilty that his mother had taken her own life? And wasn't Avi's suicide a repetition of the trauma, which strongly reinforced his feelings of guilt, thus convincing him that he truly was a murderer? If so, was it possible that David, afraid that he might destroy me as he had destroyed his mother and his son, felt that he had to leave treatment for his safety and mine?

The answers to these questions were revealed in the next session. David again began to tackle the issue of his guilt over Avi's suicide. He said, "There is something I've never told you. When Avi deserted his unit the second time, I put pressure on him to go back. I did not want a son who was a deserter. The entire course of events might have been different if I had reacted differently. We will never know."

I asked David whether he felt that my opposition to his desire to desert treatment might endanger his life. This was frighteningly similar to David's insistence that Avi not desert the army, which he felt had ultimately endangered Avi's life. David shocked me by saying, "If there is danger here, then you are in danger. I told you once that if I had a gun, I wouldn't kill myself as Avi did, I would kill someone else. Perhaps that is why you put up all these boundaries between us," he added with a grin.

We were quiet for several moments. I felt that David had unleashed his murderous aspect into the room—either he or I could be destroyed. Abandoning treatment was a mild solution compared to a violent acting out which would cause his or my own destruction. However, as a result of the elaboration of my countertransference with regard to David's feelings of guilt caused by the suicides of his son and his mother, I was no longer afraid. I had come to the realization that David's infantile unconscious wishes did not make him an actual murderer. Thus, I was able to summon my strength and say, "I think it is important that you remain in treatment and not leave at this point. Do not be afraid. Neither you nor I will be destroyed. And I hope that when we finish our work, you will be more independent and able to manage on your own."

In contrast to the first time that I had tried to stop David from abandoning treatment, this time I was successful. David arrived at the next session limping and complaining of back pain. He said, "I came today with all my pain, not in spite of it. I did not want to miss the session. Last session made me understand that you invest a lot of thought in the treatment and that there's a plan for my recovery. This was an important realization for me."

Based on the tremendous amount of work that he and I had done over the years, I succeeded in conveying to David that we could both survive his destructive impulses. My initial fear of David's aggression as well as my belief that he might have induced his son to take his own life had changed, and David was able to perceive this change. Moreover, he could also realize that I had faith in his ability to develop and grow, and that I wanted to help him separate from me once he had developed more stable psychic boundaries. The therapeutic relationship was restored and we both felt that, in spite of all the problems, our lives as well as the treatment would continue.

David was now ready to delve into his relationship with his complex internal maternal representation. My survival of his aggression in the transference enabled us to uncover and elaborate upon it. Becoming aware that he could also deeply hate his loving, nurturing mother, who had fought hard to give him life and to keep him alive when he was an infant, was extremely painful to him. For a long time in analysis he tried to cling to his idealized image of her and denied the horror of their perverse closeness. Much psychic work was needed to help David acknowledge the dark aspects of his relationship with his mother. The long, painful work of mourning and the elaboration of his hateful and destructive feelings toward her, as well as toward me in the transference, helped David achieve a greater degree of separation from his mother, thus establishing more stable psychic boundaries.

In contrast to his former wish to go to Hungary to commit suicide and unite with his mother in her grave, David now decided to travel to Budapest to see his sons from his first marriage. He was excited at the prospect and expressed the desire to write a will in which he would leave them his parents' house as an inheritance.

On his return, David reported on the encounter with his sons, which he described as very moving. We connected David's guilt for abandoning his sons with the guilt evoked by Avi's suicide. I reminded David that, in both cases, he had expressed the wish "to erase the children from his life, to live with a woman in a kind of bubble, without children and without worries." David replied, "That was only a fantasy. In reality, Avi was very important to me and I worried about him a lot. I loved and admired Avi very much." I felt that David was now better able to deal with his destructive wishes because his hatred of his son had been mitigated by his love for him. David was now able to create a boundary between fantasy and reality and could better differentiate between them.

At this stage of analysis, David's omnipotent defenses were replaced by working through his mourning and guilt over Avi. Now that he was better able to accept Avi's death, he could cry over his loss and mourn his son's talent, youth, and beauty. David felt that in losing Avi he had lost an important part of himself; he was aware that by renewing contact with his sons abroad, he was attempting to retrieve other parts of himself which were lost a long time ago.

There was a change in David's relationship with important objects in his life. He spoke about his wife with greater compassion and empathy. Their relationship improved, although he still had difficulty functioning sexually. In this regard David mentioned that he had given up watching sadomasochistic movies; he no longer felt the need for them. Although he still felt tired at times, his terrible exhaustion was gone, his blood pressure was stable, and the terrible psoriasis had healed. With the diminishing of his depression, he decided to look for work.

In my countertransference, I felt that David was more accepting of the analytic boundaries. I also felt that his aggression was under better control, which was an indication that his ego boundaries were stronger. His craving for oneness with me had diminished, thus establishing a psychic boundary between us, which enabled David to continue analysis with a more secure sense of self.

DISCUSSION

I will now use this case illustration to discuss the impact of trauma on the breaking of boundaries from a cultural perspective, based on the Holocaust experience. I will first demonstrate how the mother's Holocaust past intruded into the patient's life, affecting the mother-child relationship and the child's cognitive and emotional development. I will then examine how the patient enacted the mother's traumatic past, thus breaking boundaries between past and present, reality and fantasy, self and object. To conclude, I will discuss the impact of trauma on boundaries from a clinical perspective. I will relate how the patient's breaking of the analytic boundaries affected both treatment and analyst, and how the analyst coped with these problems.

The Impact of Trauma on Boundaries from the Cultural Perspective: The Effect on Cognitive and Emotional Development

A culture is defined as a particular society or civilization, especially one considered in relation to its ideas, its art, or its way of life (*Collins*, 1991). The Holocaust affected an entire culture. It was an unprecedented, systematic attempt to achieve "racial purity" through the extermination of innocent people. It was a cataclysmic event that changed the shape of human history forever. In this period of infamy, the boundaries between the human and the inhuman were broken. Six million of Europe's Jews were murdered, and along with them a rich and thriving culture disappeared. The Holocaust affected not only the lives of the survivors, but also the lives of second- and third-generation offspring of these victims throughout the world.

The above case illustration portrays the son of two Holocaust survivor parents who were damaged to the point that they allowed an incestuous relationship to take place between mother and son, thus breaking the boundaries between generations. The incestuous relationship involved extreme emotional and physical closeness, stopping short of intercourse, between mother and son until the son's late adolescence.

Welldon (1993) relates to the effect that trauma can have on mothers and on their relationship with their children. She suggests that the opportunity that maternity offers to have complete control of a situation creates the right preconditions for certain women, who have suffered harmful traumatic experiences, to exploit and abuse their children. In the above case, the mother related to her son as a part or prolongation of her own body, which served to counter her fear of loss and destruction by creating the illusion that she and her child would remain bound together forever.

The mother's symbiotic relationship with the patient made it extremely difficult for him to extricate himself from it and create boundaries around his self. His difficulty in separating from his mother threatened the integration of the self (Mahler et al., 1975) and created problems with his body image (Apprey, 1991; Fischer, 1991; Kramer, 1983, 1991, 1994; Steele, 1991; Brenner, 2004). The incestuous relationship, which often leads to disturbances in attachment (Bowlby, 1973), and the parent's failure to mirror (Winnicott, 1967) and reflect the child's experience (Denett, 1987; Fonagy et al., 1991), brought about several developmental failures in the patient, which I will describe briefly:

1. *Disturbed reality testing.* David regarded his molestation by his mother as an act of love rather than her narcissistic exploitation of him for her

own physical and emotional needs. He viewed their relationship as mutually beneficial (Rachman, 1989, 1997; Brenner, 2004).

2. *Identification with the victim/aggressor aspects of his mother.* In his family life, David enacted the victim aspect of his mother by playing the role of the battered child of his dominant controlling wife, thus putting her in the role of Nazi persecutor. In his masturbatory fantasies, he was the aggressive adult (the Nazi torturer) who abused the child.

3. *Adolescent suicidal strivings.* The longing to achieve a blissful union with his mother through suicide, a longing which is typical of adolescence, was a pivotal component of the patient's psychic life. The association of this longing with thoughts of suicide, or the actual suicide itself, is usually mediated by changes in ego functions, the quality of which depends greatly on the structural-cognitive development that takes place in adolescence (Ehrlich, 1978). In the above case, thoughts of achieving a blissful union with the mother through suicide had not undergone successful transformation because little had changed in the patient's concrete style of thinking since adolescence.

4. *Defective superego.* In the above case, the patient's defective superego stemmed from (a) a weak paternal introject, who was unable to erect any barriers against incest; and (b) the denial by all of the complicity fostered between mother and son in their seductive and sexual transgression, which contributed to the corruption of the superego (Blum, 1973).

5. *Perverse psychic structure.* The erasing of the differences between the generations described in this case illustration, which is typical of perversion, has been amply explored by Chasseguet-Smirgel (1978, 1984). She refers to the craving for oneness with the mother as a longing for "union with a universe without obstacles, without roughness or differences, entirely smooth, identified with a mother's belly stripped of content, an interior to which one has free access" (1996, p. 77). This phenomenon includes a return to an undifferentiated state that precedes the introduction of separation, distinction, and paternal law, and which is specific to the anal-sadistic stage to which the pervert regresses. In the above case, we observe this phenomenon in the patient's fantasies of erasing all obstacles (his father, his children, my other patients) that hindered his symbiosis with his mother/wife/therapist. In contrast to the neurotic, for whom the oedipal prohibition is accompanied by a sense of horror—a sacred prohibition as Freud (1939) calls it—of returning to the place he came from (the mother's womb) for fear of losing his hard-won identity, in the above case, this fear was absent. The patient's sexual identity was fluid; he identified both with the brutal man as well as with the submissive woman. The patient did not experience incest as a horror, but instead idealized the object of his craving.

The Reliving of the Past in the Present

For children of survivors, no matter where they live, there is no escape. There is no memory of a time when the Holocaust did not exist in their awareness. Their "remembrance" of the Holocaust is constructed out of stories— those that were spoken aloud, told and retold, as well as those that were silently borne across a bridge of generations (Axelrod, Schnipper, and Rau, 1978; Barocas and Barocas, 1973; Kestenberg, 1972; Klein, 1971; Laufer, 1973; Lipkowitz, 1973; Rakoff, 1966; Sonnenberg, 1974; Laub and Auerhahn, 1993; Auerhahn and Laub, 1998). This remembrance marks those who know it as secret bearers (Micheels, 1985). The children who become burdened by memories that are not their own (Auerhahn and Prelinger, 1983; Fresco, 1984) often echo the drama existing in their parents' inner world by enacting it in their current life (Krell, 1979; Phillips, 1978; Laub and Auerhahn, 1984; Kogan, 1995, 1998, 2003). These violent enactments are often the result of death wishes, leading them to expose themselves to situations of external danger (Kogan, 2002).

The above case study reveals the secret perverse world of the patient, in which the violent Holocaust past of the mother intruded into his present life and broke boundaries between past and present, fantasy and reality, self and object, as mentioned above. I will discuss: (a) The revivification of the mother's Holocaust past through the patient's fantasies and enactments and (b) The interplay between present trauma (the son's suicide) and past trauma (the mother's suicide) and its impact on the patient.

The Revivification of the Mother's Holocaust Past through the Patient's Fantasies and Enactments

The mother's "mythos of survival" (Kris, 1956; Klein, 1981; Kogan, 1995), which consisted of her unconscious conflicting emotions and wishes regarding life and death, permeated her son's boundaries, in a process of projection-intojection. The conflict between the patient's subsequent life and death wishes was demonstrated, for example, by his suicidal wish to jump off a tall building. David attempted to counter this wish by infusing his inner life with his perverse fantasy of brutally torturing big, strong women. This fantasy was actually a "manic defense" (Winnicott, 1935; Klein 1935), which served to overcome his death wishes.

The conflict between life and death forces was also revealed in the patient's flirtation with danger. By volunteering to serve in a special army reserve unit during the Gulf War, and being among the first to arrive at the site where a scud missile had landed to determine whether it had a chemical or biological warhead, David was attempting to come close to death in order to overcome it (Kogan, 1995, 1998, 2002).

The pull between the forces of life and death stemmed also from the way in which the patient unconsciously perceived the life-giving sexual relationship between his damaged ("dead") parents. Seeing it as "empty" (Ogden, 1966) and murderous (David's description of "the acidic environment of a woman's body," above), he fantasized that he had already died in his mother's belly. Flirting with danger by entering the area where the missiles had landed could signify an attempt to infuse life into an empty primal scene as well as into himself.

The conflict between life and death forces was further expressed in the patient's psychosomatic diseases. David's body became the stage upon which the drama of the past was being acted out. His various psychosomatic conditions (psoriasis, high blood pressure, impotence, an ulcer), which represented his self-destructiveness, may also be regarded as an enactment upon his own body of his unconscious fantasies regarding his mother's traumatic past. These fantasies were acted out by his associating parts of his body with the offending object (the Nazi aggressor) and then attacking them brutally.

The antifertility treatment which the patient's mother had undergone during the Holocaust, which may have been eroticized by him, could have served as a source for his masturbatory fantasies. In this fantasy he played the role of the brutal male (the Nazi torturer) who performs the antifertility treatment, as well as the female victim who underwent it. His impotence may be regarded as a form of symbolic self-castration, a punishment for his sexual wishes toward the mother embodied in these fantasies.

The Interplay between Present Trauma (the Son's Suicide) and Past Trauma (the Mother's Suicide) and Its Impact on the Patient

To assess how the trauma of the son's suicide affected the patient, we first have to understand how the present trauma was associated by him with his underlying destructive fantasies (of erasing all obstructions to his merging with his wife/mother), and then how the present trauma affected the memory of the past (in this case, how the son's suicide superimposed itself on the mother's suicide).

Greenacre (1967) maintains that, in situations where actual traumatic experiences are associated with an underlying fantasy stemming from difficult experiences, the impact of the actual trauma is more intense, and the tendency to fixation is greater than in instances where life experiences are bland and incidental. David associated the loss of his son with his aggressive wish of ridding himself of any obstacles to his fusion with his wife/mother. Since he had regarded his son as one of these obstacles, he became convinced he was his son's murderer, the son's suicide perceived by him as the actualization of his omnipotent destructive fantasies. This led to unbearable feelings of pain and guilt, which impaired his work of mourning and caused him to turn his aggression against his own self, making him depressed and suicidal.

In the above illustration, his son's suicide reinforced the patient's feelings of guilt toward his mother, which he had harbored over a prolonged period of time. There is no time in the unconscious (Freud, 1915), only the articulation of meanings (Schaeffer, 1980). Past and present merge in the unconscious, so that meanings that were, still are, and the meanings that are, affect and change those that were (Loftus and Loftus, 1980). The psychoanalytic model of trauma is thus composed of two events: a later event that causes the revivification of an original event, which only then becomes traumatic (Laplanche and Pontalis, 1967).

David felt in his unconscious fantasy that his conception and birth had led to his mother's illness, suffering, and eventual suicide. This fantasy took on traumatic proportions when reality gave it credence through his son's self-destructive act. David associated his fantasy of being responsible for the trauma of his son's suicide with his underlying fantasy of responsibility for his mother's suicide, thus becoming convinced that he was his mother's murderer. The interplay between the past trauma and the present trauma reinforced each of the traumas, convincing the patient that he was the murderer in both.

The Impact of Trauma on Boundaries from the Clinical Perspective

In their famous book *Boundaries and Boundary Violation*, Gabbard and Lester (1995) state that "a central paradox of the analytic situation is that professional boundaries must be maintained so that both participants have the freedom to cross them psychologically" (p. 42). In the above case illustration, it was difficult at times to maintain the professional (external) boundaries that constitute the analytic frame, within which "the patient's needs, wishes and demands for transcendence and transgression unfold and are understood, renounced, modified and rechanneled" (Akhtar, 1999, p. 116).

I will discuss the clinical breaking of boundaries from two aspects: (1) how the patient's attacking the treatment and his breaking of analytic boundaries affected the analyst; and (2) how traumatic reality, when it intruded into analysis and broke the boundaries between the internal and external world, affected the treatment. In both instances, I will discuss how I coped with these problems.

Analysts are continuously attending to the difference between what is transpiring inside the patient and what is transpiring inside themselves. The analytic boundaries facilitate this process by functioning as interpersonal boundaries. The analyst may thus regard them as an extension of his own outer ego boundaries (Epstein, 1994), and if the analytic frame is attacked, the analyst might experience it as an attack upon himself.

Although my patient would at times appear depressed and helpless, his frequent breaking of the analytic boundaries caused me to experience him as a powerful, menacing figure who could destroy me as well as the treatment. My fear of him helped me realize that beneath his game playing in his relationship with me lay a terrible destructiveness, which included his wish to devour me, a hatred of my separateness and autonomy, and a desire to destroy them. I experienced his breaking of interpersonal boundaries as a threat to my safety. There were points in analysis when I asked myself whether I could continue analytic work with this violent, frightening patient. It was only by making my internal boundaries permeable to my countertransference feelings, so that I could be in touch with them and work them through, that I was able to understand my patient and thus become less afraid of him. Working through my shock and amazement when the patient broke the analytical boundaries, I became aware of the patient's own fear of his uncontrollable aggression and of his possible fragmentation. Elaborating upon my anger over his attempt to have sadistic omnipotent control over me by breaking the boundaries of the analytic setup, I understood that this was his way of defending himself against the danger of fusing with me and losing his own self in the process. An analysis of my feelings of being under constant stress in this treatment helped me realize that the patient, as the child of two damaged parents, had lived in a state of chronic "strain trauma" (Kris, 1956) from an early age. Thus, perhaps he was letting me feel the strain he had experienced in his childhood, when he had been frequently and chronically flooded with anger and sexual arousal without adequate parental protection for modulating these affects.

The craving to merge with his mother, which persisted throughout the patient's life, was expressed in analysis through "transference perversion" (Etchegoyen, 1977). This type of transference includes a narcissistic object relation, by means of which the patient attempts to construct a delusional subject-object unity, as well as to break analytic boundaries, with the aim of provoking fear and arousal in the analyst. To deal with this "transference perversion," I had to develop a unique form of psychoanalytic empathy toward my patient. This included, in Kernberg's (1995) terms, creating a "thickness" in the treatment's external boundaries by firmly maintaining the therapeutic role, and creating an optimal "thinness" in my internal boundary, that is, an openness to explore unconscious processes and countertransference feelings.

Analyzing my countertransference feelings, I realized that in addition to the patient's breaking of analytic boundaries, the overwhelming reality of his son's suicide intruded so violently into the treatment that it erased the boundaries between fantasy and reality for both members of the analytic dyad. I felt threatened because I myself perceived the patient as a monstrous father who might have induced his son to commit suicide, thus fulfilling his unconscious aggressive wishes of erasing his son from his life. My associations with regard to the patient revolved around the legend of Chronos, the

Greek god who swallowed his children, or Saturn, another Greek god identified with Chronos, whom Goya painted swallowing one of his children. These associations made me aware of how appalled I was by the patient and afraid of his murderous impulses, which I felt had been realized by his son's suicide. Only by working through my feelings did I understand that my own ability to symbolize, as well as the patient's, had been greatly impaired by the traumatic reality of his son's suicide. It was essential that both the patient and myself understand that his unconscious aggressive wishes toward his son (or toward me in the transference) did not necessarily turn him into a murderer. Recovering my ability to symbolize and relate to his murderous wishes as an infantile fantasy and not a reality created a new analytic space in which the patient was no longer a threat to me, and in which we could work through the mourning for his son as well as for his mother.

In this newly created analytic space I was able to show the patient that his breaking of the analytic boundaries, his need to control the situation and destroy the asymmetry between us, his eroticization of the relationship, not only served to rid himself of his painful feelings regarding his son but also to rid himself of me in my role as therapist. David attacked the treatment because therapy itself was experienced by him as a boundary, a "third," that interfered with the dyadic incestuous relationship he wanted to create. My surviving his attacks helped David to better differentiate between fantasy and reality and feel less threatened by his infantile aggressive and libidinal strivings (Kogan, 1990, 1995). Working through the feelings of pain and guilt for his lost son helped David disassociate these feelings from the guilt and unresolved mourning for his dead mother, and facilitated the restoration of boundaries between fantasy and reality, past and present, self and object. After years of hard work, the patient emerged from the treatment with a better differentiated self and renewed life forces.

In this regard, I find Joseph's (1982) eloquent statement relevant: "I have described . . . the pull of death instincts, the pull towards near-death, a kind of mental or physical brinkmanship in which the seeing of the self in this dilemma, unable to be helped, is an essential aspect. It is however important to consider where the pull towards life and sanity is. I believe that this part of the patient is located in the analyst" (p. 128). I believe that in this case, the pull toward life and sanity that my patient located in me was one of the crucial aspects of this treatment.

REFERENCES

Akhtar, S. (1999). *Immigration and Identity—Turmoil, Treatment and Transformation*. Northvale, NJ: Jason Aronson.

Apprey, M. (1991). Psychical transformations by a child of incest. In *The Trauma of Transgression*, eds. S. Kramer and S. Akhtar, pp. 115–148. Northvale, NJ: Jason Aronson.

Auerhahn, N. C., and Laub, D. (1998). Intergenerational memory of the Holocaust. In *International Handbook of Multigenerational Legacies of Trauma*, ed. Y. Danieli, pp. 21–43. New York: Plenum Press.

Auerhahn, N. C., and Prelinger, E. (1983). Repetition in the concentration camp survivor and her child. *International Review of Psychoanalysis* 10:31–46.

Axelrod, S., Schnipper, O. L., and Rau, J. H. (1978). Hospitalized offspring of Holocaust survivors: Problems and dynamics. Paper presented at the Annual Meeting of the American Psychiatric Association, May 1978.

Barocas, H. A., and Barocas, C. B. (1973). Manifestations of concentration camp effects on the second generation. *American Journal of Psychiatry* 130:8201–8204.

Blum, H. P. (1973). The concept of eroticized transference. *Journal of the American Psychoanalytic Association* 21:61–76.

Bowlby, J. (1973). *Attachment and Loss, Vol. 2: Separation: Anxiety and Anger.* New York: Basic.

Brenner, I. (2004). *Psychic Trauma—Dynamics, Symptoms and Treatment.* Lanham, MD: Jason Aronson.

Chasseguet-Smirgel, J. (1978). Reflections on the connections between sadism and perversion. *International Journal of Psychoanalysis* 59:27–35.

———. (1984). *Creativity and Perversion.* New York: Norton.

———. (1996). The archaic matrix of the Oedipus Complex. In *Sexuality and Mind—The Role of the Father and the Mother in the Psyche*, pp. 74–92. New York: New York University Press.

Collins Cobuild English Language Dictionary. London, 1991.

Denett, D. (1987). *The Intentional Stance.* Cambridge, MA: MIT Press.

Ehrlich, S. (1978). Adolescent suicide—maternal longing and cognitive development. *Psychoanalytic Study of the Child* 33:261–277.

Epstein, R. S. (1994). *Keeping Boundaries—Maintaining Safety and Integrity in the Psychotherapeutic Process.* Washington, DC: American Psychiatric Press.

Etchegoyen, R. H. (1977). Perversion of transference: Theoretical and technical aspects. In *Prácticas Psicoanalíticas Comparadas en las Psicosis*, ed. L. Grinberg, pp. 58–83. Buenos Aires: Piados.

Fischer, R. M. S. (1991). The unresolved rapprochement crisis: An important constituent of the incest experience. In *The Trauma of Transgression*, eds. S. Kramer and S. Akhtar, pp. 39–56. Northvale, NJ: Jason Aronson.

Fonagy, P., Steele, M., Moran, G., et al. (1991). The capacity for understanding mental states: The reflective self in parent and child and its significance for security of attachment. *Infant Mental Health Journal* 13:200–217.

Fresco, N. (1984). Remembering the unknown. *International Review of Psychoanalysis* 11:417–427.

Freud, S. (1911). Formulations on the two principles of mental functioning. *Standard Edition* 12:213–237.

———. (1915). The unconscious. *Standard Edition* 14:159–237.

———. (1939). Moses and monotheism. *Standard Edition* 23:1–139.

Gabbard, G. O., and Lester, E. P. (1995). *Boundaries and Boundary Violations in Psychoanalysis.* Washington, DC: American Psychiatric Publishing, Inc.

Greenacre, P. (1967). The influence of infantile trauma on genetic patterns. In *Psychic Trauma*, ed. S. S. Furst, pp. 260–299. New York: Basic.

Grinberg, L. (1964). Two kinds of guilt: Their relations with normal and pathological aspects of mourning. *International Journal of Psychoanalysis* 45:3671.

Joseph, B. (1982). Addiction to near-death. In *Psychic Equilibrium and Psychic Change*, eds. M. Feldman and E. Bott Spillius, pp. 127–139. London: Tavistock/Routledge, 1991.

Kernberg, O. F. (1995). Foreword. In *Boundaries and Boundaries Violations.* Washington, DC: American Psychiatric Publishing, Inc.

Kestenberg, J. S. (1972). How children remember and parents forget. *International Journal of Psychoanalysis and Psychotherapy* 1–2:103–123.

Klein, H. (1971). Families of Holocaust survivors in the kibbutz: Psychological studies. In *Psychic Traumatisation: After-Effects in Individuals and Communities.* Boston: Little, Brown.

———. (1981). Yale Symposium on the Holocaust. *Proceedings*, September 1981.

Klein, M. (1935). A contribution to the psychogenesis of manic-depressive states. In *Love, Guilt and Reparation, and Other Works, 1921–1945*, pp. 262–289. New York: Free Press, 1975.

Kogan, I. (1990). A journey to pain. *International Journal of Psychoanalysis* 1:629–540.

———. (1995). *The Cry of Mute Children—A Psychoanalytic Perspective of the Second Generation of the Holocaust.* London: Free Association Books.

———. (1998). The black hole of dread: The psychic reality of children of Holocaust survivors. In *Even Paranoids Have Enemies: New Perspectives on Paranoia and Persecution*, eds. J. H. Berke, S. Pierides, A. Sobbaddini, and S. Schneider, pp. 47–59. London: Routledge.

———. (2002). "Enactment" in the lives and treatment of Holocaust survivors' offspring. *Psychoanalytic Quarterly* LXXI(2):251–273.

———. (2003). On being a dead, beloved child. *Psychoanalytic Quarterly* LXXII(3):727–767.

Kramer, S. (1983). Object-coercive doubting: A pathological defense response to maternal incest. *Journal of the American Psychoanalytic Association* 31:325–351.

———. (1991). Psychopathological effects of incest. In *The Trauma of Transgression*, eds. S. Kramer and S. Akhtar, pp. 1–12. Northvale, NJ: Jason Aronson.

———. (1994). Further considerations of somatic and cognitive residues of incest. In *Victims of Abuse*, ed. A. Sugarman, pp. 69–96. Madison, CT: International Universities Press.

Krell, R. (1979). Holocaust families: The survivors and their children. *Comprehensive Psychiatry* 20(6):560–567.

Kris, E. (1956). The personal myth: A problem in psychoanalytic technique. *Journal of the American Psychoanalytic Association* 4:653–681.

Laplanche, J., and Pontalis, J. P. (1967). *The Language of Psychoanalysis.* New York: Norton, 1973.

Laub, D., and Auerhahn, N. C. (1984). Reverberations of genocide: Its expression in the conscious and unconscious of post-Holocaust generations. In *Psychoanalytic*

Reflections of the Holocaust: Selected Essays, eds. S. A. Luel and P. Marcus, pp. 151–167. Denver, CO: Ktav Publishing House.

———. (1993). Knowing and not knowing psychic trauma: Forms of traumatic memory. *International Journal of Psychoanalysis* 74:287–302.

Laufer, M. (1973). The analysis of a child of survivors. In *The Child in His Family: The Impact of Disease and Death*, eds. E. J. Anthony and C. Koupernik, 2:363–373. New York: Wiley.

Lipkowitz, M. H. (1973). The child of two survivors: The report of an unsuccessful therapy. *Israeli Annals of Psychiatry and Related Discliplines* 11:2.

Loftus, E. F., and Loftus, G. R. (1980). On the permanence of stored information on the human brain. *American Psychologist* 5:405–420.

Mahler, M. S., Pine, F., and Bergman, A. (1975). *The Psychological Birth of the Human Infant*. New York: Basic Books.

McLaughlin, J. (1995). Touching limits in the analytic dyad. *Psychoanalytic Quarterly* 64:433–465.

Micheels, L. J. (1985). Bearer of the secret. *Psychoanalytic Inquiry* 5:21–30.

Ogden, T. H. (1966). The perverse subject of analysis. *Journal of the American Psychoanalytic Association* 44:1121–1146.

Phillips, R. (1978). Impact of Nazi Holocaust on children of survivors. *American Journal of Psychotherapy* 32:370–377.

Rachman, A. W. (1989). Confusion of tongues: The Ferenczion metaphor for childhood seduction and emotional trauma. *Journal of the American Academy of Psychoanalysis* 17:182–205.

———. (1997). The suppression and censorship of Ferenczi's "confusion of tongues" paper. *Psychoanalytic Inquiry* 17:459–485.

Rakoff, V. (1966). Long-term effects of the concentration camp experience. *Viewpoints* 1:17–21.

Schaeffer, S. F. (1980). The unreality of realism. *Critical Inquiry* 6:727–738.

Sonnenberg, S. M. (1974). Children of survivors: Workshop report. *Journal of the American Psychoanalytic Association* 22:200–204.

Steele, B. E. (1991). The psychopathology of incest participants. In *The Trauma of Transgression*, eds. S. Kramer and S. Akhtar, pp. 13–38. Northvale, NJ: Jason Aronson.

Stoller, R. (1975). *Perversion*. New York: Pantheon.

Welldon, E. V. (1993). *Madre, Virgin, Puta. Idealizacion y enigrecion de la Maternidad (Mother, Madonna, Whore. The idealization and denigration of motherhood)*. Madrid: Siglo XXI.

Winnicott, D. W. (1935). The manic defense. In *Collected Papers: Through Pediatrics to Psychoanalysis*, pp. 129–144. London: Tavistock.

———. (1967). Mirror-role of the mother and family in child development. In *The Predicament of the Family: A Psychoanalytic Symposium*, ed. P. Lomas, pp. 26–33. London: Hogarth Press.

———. (1971). The use of an object and relating through identification. In *Playing and Reality*, pp. 101–112. London: Tavistock.

7

Experiencing Oneness—Pathological Pursuit or Normal Necessity? Discussion of Kogan's Chapter, "Breaking of Boundaries and Craving for Oneness"

Salman Akhtar, M.D.

Dr. Ilany Kogan, for whose theoretical depth, clinical sophistication, and literary elegance I have the utmost respect, has offered us a rich and powerful contribution here. Simultaneously engaging and complex, her work elucidates how trauma results in breakdown of generational boundaries and how the offspring of boundaryless parents can get involved in a desperate and doomed lifelong search for oneness. Besides thus highlighting theoretical links between transgenerational transmission of trauma and the formation of ego boundaries, Dr. Kogan's contribution—centering on the analysis of a middle-aged son of Holocaust survivors—also offers us a glimpse of how an exceptionally talented and skillful analyst works under difficult and testing situations. Dr. Kogan has given us a gem and we owe a debt of gratitude to her.

Therefore I comment upon her contribution with hesitation. My task is made difficult because I not only agree with her ideas but I admire them. At the same time, it would be dishonest to say that I do not have any questions, additional notions, and alternate perspectives on an individual's search for oneness. In presenting these ideas and in commenting upon Dr. Kogan's paper, I will divide my remarks into four sections: theory, technique, transcultural aspects, and some existential realms that seem inoptimally addressed not only by Dr. Kogan's paper but perhaps also by psychoanalytic theory in general.

SOME MATTERS OF THEORY

Dr. Kogan begins her contribution by surveying the literature upon the concept of boundaries. She cites Freud (1911), Federn (1952), Jacobson (1964), Hartmann (1969), Anzieu (1992), and Gabbard and Lester (1995) and brings forth the concepts of *ego boundaries* (which on the inside separate the ego from the fantasy world and on the outside from reality), the *boundaries between self and object representations* (which help retain the intrapsychic difference in the experience of the self and its internal objects), *interpersonal boundaries* (which regulate the extent of intimacy possible without the dread of fusion and separateness needed without the specter of lonely despair), and *skin envelope* (which, metaphorically, contains psychic experience and precludes massive projections and inner-outer confusion). Dr. Kogan then adds the dimension of time to the concept of boundaries. Such *temporal boundaries* help distinguish past from present. She emphasizes their separating functions but pays less attention, it seems, to the need for permeability in this membrane. After all, a certain "continuity amidst change" (Erikson, 1959) is a hallmark of healthy identity. While we do not need to be prisoners of our past, we do require connections with our history, without which we are temporally hollow and uncannily contemporaneous. To say that a meaningful self should have temporal boundaries is not enough without qualifying that such boundaries need to be permeable.

Similarly, when Dr. Kogan outlines the impact of transgenerational trauma upon the formation of boundaries, I find her ideas congenial but incomplete. Dr. Kogan states that the symbiotic relationship between her patient and his mother led to many psychopathological developments. These included deficient reality testing, identification with the victim-aggressor aspects of his mother's self, suicidal inclination during adolescence, weak superego, and a perverse character organization where transgressing boundaries was suffused with manic triumph and not subject to neurotic dread. I find Dr. Kogan's formulation convincing. However, I feel that there is insufficient distinction here between the psychopathological results and how they actually come about. It is my understanding—both from the material provided by Dr. Kogan and from my own clinical experience—that traumatized parents are unable to help their children develop adequate boundaries in five different ways that often operate in unison:

1. *Overidentifying with the child:* Traumatized parents overidentify with the inherent fragility of their child. As a result, they feel anxious in frustrating the child. Consequently, the child fails to develop an adequate distinction between realistic and wishful states of the self (and their respective relatedness with objects).

2. *Mistaking ordinary parental control with cruelty:* Being chronically (even if unconsciously) enraged, traumatized parents are vulnerable to confusing their legitimate and needed assertion with destructive aggression. Ordinary parental control becomes akin to cruelty in their mind. This renders them unable to set limits for their child who, as a result, is saddled with unbridled greed and omnipotence.

3. *Finding it difficult to exclude the child from any activity or sphere of life:* Traumatized parents have frequently experienced agonizing marginalization and "catastrophic aloneness" (Grand, 2000). In a naïve attempt to reverse this trauma, they often include their child in all spheres of their lives. Establishing generational boundaries is difficult for them; primal scene either goes blank or becomes a public scene. In either case, the child becomes oedipally triumphant and cocky. The fact that the parental marriage in such instances is often inappropriate (e.g., with a marked sociocultural or age difference between partners) also facilitates such a transgressive bent on the offspring's part.

4. *Spoiling the child due to envy:* Traumatized parents envy their offspring for their more fortunate realities. This envy leads them to spoil the child's normal growth. The spoiling effort may be directly hostile or may exert their destruction effects via tenacious reaction formation on the patient's part. Either way, healthy boundary formations is precluded.

5. *Reenacting one's own traumas:* Traumatized parents identify with their aggressors and enact scenarios of sadistic destruction of boundaries with their offspring. Under the sway of instinctually driven repetition—compulsion—they relive, again and again, the tormented moments when their own "protective shield" (Freud, 1895) was broken; only this time they are in the perpetrator's role.

These five mechanisms do not find explicit mention in Dr. Kogan's paper though their presence is felt in her clinical material.

Two other theoretical issues warrant mention before we move on to psychoanalytic technique. The first refers to Dr. Kogan's view of her patient's psychosomatic problems and the second to her inattention toward the boundaries between psychic structures. Regarding the first, it seems that Dr. Kogan subscribes to the specificity theory of psychosomatics. In other words, particular symptoms represent to her particular fantasies being enacted upon the body. This, while occasionally true, is by and large an outdated mode of thinking. Gone are the days when peptic ulcer suggested unmet oral strivings, bronchial asthma a desperate cry for rescue, and hypertension a sign of suppressed rage. Clinical experience has failed to validate this type of linear conceptualization. Instead, psychosomatic outbreaks are now seen as nonspecific manifestations of chronically unmentalized inward aggression; Gaddini's

(1972) notion about the third fate of the death instinct (the first being its externalization leading to the creation of persecutory objects and the second being its binding by life instinct resulting in primary masochism) apply to this very point. Autoimmunity is the mindless key to the puzzle where the choice of the suffering organ is due to hereditary, constitutional, and coincidental factors and not unconscious fantasy.

The second theoretical concern pertains to the boundaries between intrapsychic structures. This is not adequately discussed by Dr. Kogan. While Freud's (1900, 1915) topographic model and Sandler and Sandler's (1983) "three box model" rest upon the notion of such boundaries, what I have in mind here are the boundaries that exist between id and ego, ego and superego, ego and ego ideal, and id and superego. Rupture of these boundaries causes problems and such problems are frequently in traumatized individuals' children. Id-ego merger causes an instinctualized ego. Ego-superego merger causes "identification with the superego" (Klein, 1975) and tendency toward moralizing and domination. Ego and ego-ideal merger creates a narcissistic and "perverse character" (Chassegeut-Smirgel, 1984). Id-superego collusion causes a fantastic and pressured superego which makes its demands in a cyclical manner like id. And so on. While no paper can have everything, one does wish that Dr. Kogan would have included even an *en passant* remark on such structural blurrings, especially since her clinical material gives ample testimony to the veracity of such phenomena.

THREE ASPECTS OF TECHNIQUE

The clinical material presented by Dr. Kogan is vivid, poignant, occasionally shocking, but above all clinically impressive and instructive. Her technical handling of the associative links, nonverbal clues, dreams, in-office enactments, and extra-analytic encounters is superb. We see a master clinician at work here. There is elaboration and analysis of transference as well as description and management of countertransference. The analyst's internal reflections facilitate her deconstructive efforts toward interactive elements of the clinical work. There are pauses, hesitations, letting things evolve, and rolling with the punches as well as confrontation, reality testing, "affirmative interventions" (Killingmo, 1989), reconstructions, and genetic interpretations. Dr. Kogan's technique deftly combines the ever-needed "survival of the object" (Winnicott, 1962) with an incisive understanding of what is being hidden by what is being revealed. Support and even reassurance find their way in her work which is nonetheless focused on the unconscious determinants of the patient's anguish and his manic efforts to ward it off. Dr. Kogan's style has both the prose of Freud and the music of Ferenczi. In bridging the two, her style acquires the status of poetry. This is psychoanalytic work at its best and though its beauty lies in a harmonious gestalt, three aspects need special mention, namely survival, vision, and faith.

1. Survival: A deeply sustained aspect of Dr. Kogan's approach is that of "survival." Winnicott's 1962 declaration that a mother must "survive" (i.e., retain and/or recover the maternal function of holding, containing, being there, facilitating authentic unfolding of her child's self, etc.) finds its clinical counterpart in Dr. Kogan's work. Finding herself confronted with a patient who makes extraordinary and outrageous intrusions into her psychophysical space, she repeatedly salvages her analytic ego. Her patient touches her and while she is disturbed, her technical virtuosity remains unwavering. His son commits suicide and all sort of dynamic versions of it appear in the analytic chamber, some quite paranoid, but analysis goes on. The analyst suffers a personal loss in the form of her father's death and is doubly shocked when the patient shows up at his *shiva* (the patient even talks to the analyst's adult son). Throughout these impingements upon the analytic frame, the analyst bounces back from overwhelming emotions to analytic introspection leading to interpretation, reconstruction, and other types of analytic interventions. Never does the analyst give up on the patient and never does she give up on the analysis. The analyst "survives" and so does her analytic function.

2. Vision: The second element of Dr. Kogan's technique is what I would, for the lack of a better term, call "vision." Building upon Freud's (1913) analogy of the analyst as a sculptor who sees a shape hidden in a rock and upon Loewald's (1960) notion that the analyst helps the patient realize his or her potential by seeing them first, Dr. Kogan's maintains a future-oriented approach that is in deep intuitive contact with her patient's dormant capacities. This strengthens her ability to "survive" and also helps her patient to perceive that there is a "plan" for his treatment. It also allows Dr. Kogan to tell the patient that something he's able to feel or bear is a sign of progress. And it gives her the confidence to state: "Do not be afraid. Neither you nor I will be destroyed. And I hope when we finish our work, you will be more independent and able to manage on your own." These are developmentally oriented interventions that relieve the patient's anxiety and allow him to have a glimpse of a better future. It is such attitude and the associated conviction that human development is a lifelong process (see also Pine 1997 in this regard) that I am calling her "vision." As we observe Dr. Kogan's clinical work, we see that her mind is integrating the past, her heart is involved in the present, and her eyes remain on the future.

3. Faith: The final element in Dr. Kogan's approach is that of faith. This illusive concept had been implicit in Benedek's (1938) "confident expectation" and Erikson's (1959) "basic trust." However, it was Bion (1970) who explicitly addressed this issue. According to him, the "act of faith" responds to the gap between the handed-down theory and the reality of the clinical hour. He states that it is through the act of faith that "one can 'see', 'hear', and 'feel' the mental phenomenon of whose reality no practicing psycho-analyst has any doubt though he can not have with any accuracy represent them by existing formulations" (pp. 57–58). More recently, Neri (2005) has elucidated the intricate connections between trust and faith, noting that both result from a lengthy process of "internal work" (p. 82). He emphasizes that when a patient asks whether his suffering will ever end, he is imploring the analyst to demonstrate "a *faith* in his potential for, and right to, a satisfactory existence" (p. 82, emphasis added). In Dr. Kogan's work, this matter appears to be in the forefront of technique. She reminds us of Joseph's 1982 powerful statement:

> I have described . . . the pull of death instincts towards near-death, a kind of mental and physical brinksmanship in which the seeing of the self in this dilemma, unable to be helped is an essential element. It is however to consider when the pull towards life and sanity is. I believe this part of the patient is located in the analyst (p. 128).

This "part of the patient" presumably gets deposited in the analyst by the process of "positive projective identification" (Klein, 1946; Hamilton, 1986; Akhtar, 1995, pp. 57–58). A formulation of this sort seems plausible and elegant. However, it leaves no space for the *analyst's* work-ego and inherent "goodness" contributing to the "pull towards life and sanity." It also fails to address that such benevolence, even if located in the analyst, might be an intersubjectively co-created phenomenon. Take the following clinical example:

> Sarah Green, a 45-year-old librarian made an appointment to see me upon her sister's insistence. She appeared overwhelmed with pain at the break up of a romantic relationship. Having lived alone most of her life, she found this belated attachment profoundly significant. The man she was involved with was married. He abruptly left her saying that he could no longer continue cheating on his wife. She was destroyed. Heartbroken, she came to see me.
>
> We began the first hour of consultation in a customary history-taking way. However, within 20 minutes of the session, she announced that she had decided to blow her head off with a gun which she had bought earlier that day. Alarmed by the earnestness of her tone, I suggested that we take immediate steps to get the gun removed from her apartment, obtain some collateral information regarding the extent of her depression, and consider beginning our work on an in-patient basis. The patient reacted sharply to my suggestion and, refusing to let me contact her sister who could remove the gun, got up to leave the office. At this point, I said to her, "Look, everybody gets about 10 candles worth of life and inside you eight have already gone off. The wind is blowing hard and to protect the remaining two candles, you came here and put them in my heart. Now, since you have enlisted me for this purpose, it is my duty to keep these two candles protected from the wind. When the storm settles, I will return them to you so that you can light the other eight candles back with their help."

Without going further into the clinical process, I want to raise one question. Where did this image of 10 candles come from? Was it solely a product of my mind? Did the patient's being Jewish play a role in the creation of this menorah-like image? But wait. A menorah has only nine candles while the one I imagined had 10? What did the extra, 10th candle signify? Was it simply a matter of cultural ignorance on my part? Could it have reflected an obsessional propensity of mine toward evenness? Or, did the "well-balanced" menorah (with five candles on each side) come from an Indian aesthetic idiom emphasizing the motif of symmetry? If so, the 10 candle menorah needs to be seen as a Jewish-Indian co-creation!

Clinical material of this sort suggests that the "pull towards life and sanity" that Drs. Joseph and Kogan talk about is most likely a force that combines the patient's repudiated good internal objects with the analyst's firmly anchored benevolence (see also the case of Mr. D in Kramer and Akhtar, 1988). The analyst has "faith." The patient, like an apprentice, lives on "borrowed faith" (Akhtar, 1992a, p. 325) till developing confidence in his own capacities. Later both parties recognize (with amused tenderness) that the faith they somehow retained in their work was a product of their mutuality.

THE CULTURAL DIMENSION

Culture also plays an important role in the realm of interpersonal boundaries and craving for oneness. While not mentioned in Dr. Kogan's chapter, this variable goes a long way in determining how close or distant well-adjusted individuals may be from each other (Akhtar, 1992a). Compare the Anglo-Saxon and Germanic separateness and autonomy with Mediterranean, Latin American, and South-East Asian interpersonal fluidity and communal self and you will understand what I am talking about. The degree to which a distinct, clearly demarcated, self-observing self—the central subject of psychoanalysis—exists in different cultures varies to say the least (Akhtar, 1999; Roland, 1988). Consequently, the issue of oneness is to be viewed differently in different cultures. Craving for oneness, deemed pathological in one cultural setting, might fall within normative range of human strivings in another environment. In the latter, desire for separateness and autonomy might raise clinical eyebrows.

A corollary of such thinking is that besides the well-recognized sexual, narcissistic, and aggressive boundary violations in the clinical setting (Gabbard and Lester, 1995), there might be *cultural boundary violations* whereby the analyst imposes his or her values and notions regarding a wide range of matters (e.g., how often should an adult offspring call his out of town mother on the phone, should premarital sex be a necessary step before deciding to marry) upon the analysand, causing the latter to suffer narcissistic confusion and iatrogenic conflict. More common are cultural boundary violations caused by the analyst's ignoring that such boundaries even exist. This happens when immigrant and racially different patients are analyzed with no attention at all to their cultural backgrounds. Such illusory clinical "oneness" ends up harming the analysand and, in the long run, does disservice to the profession of psychoanalysis itself.

TWO EXISTENTIAL QUESTIONS

Permit me now to raise two other points regarding the experience of "oneness." The first pertains to the relatively restricted manner in which Dr. Kogan defines this phenomenon. She talks of oneness as the desired, imagined, dreaded, and/or desperately pursued fusion of the self and the other. I have no difficulty with this. But I think such emphasis upon the search for *oneness with the other* does not take into account that developmentally prior experiences of oneness might already lie dormant in the psychic structure. Therefore, it might be less a matter of *finding* them than of *reviving* them in adult life. Moreover, the emphasis upon *oneness with the other* overlooks another type of oneness, i.e., *oneness within oneself.* As human beings, we are always divided, forever split into parts and compartments. When we are sons and daughters, we are not husbands and wives. When we are husbands and wives, we are not brothers or sisters. When we are in public, we leave our private self behind, and when we retreat into private reverie, our external self slips out of hand. A friend stops being a surgeon at home and a surgeon ceases to be a friend upon entering the operation theater. Unlike a cat or dog or bird or tortoise or giraffe, we are hardly present anywhere with our full selves. This leaves us chronically frustrated. As a result, we strive to find states that help us become one within ourselves. I find such harmony while writing. Others might have different avenues. Regardless of the particular modality one takes to reach it, this type of "oneness" is perhaps even more important for psychoanalytic reflection. For some reason, it is not mentioned in Dr. Kogan's paper.

This leads me to my second point, that in Dr. Kogan's conceptualization, striving for "oneness" is a bit suspect. It is to be looked at with concern, if not alarm. Let me put it flatly: in her view, the search for oneness is pathological. This is certainly possible. But is it always so? Are there no healthy forms of this desire? No ego-replenishing types and extents of oneness? What about our psychic state during sexual orgasm? What about dreamless sleep? What about rapt absorption in physical exercise, writing, and religious meditation? What about the longing for oneness with the universe via death in old age? And, what about trial identification and empathy, which are the bread and butter of a working analyst? To my mind, all these states involve transient, mind-enhancing, and relationship-strengthening experiences of "oneness." There must be a reason why Dr. Kogan has not found it congenial to include them in her otherwise comprehensive contribution. I do not know that reason. What I do know is that symbiosis and individuation are two poles between which an individual oscillates throughout life (Mahler et al., 1975) and to idealize one at the cost of the other oversimplifies human experience. Mahler (1972) traces it back to early childhood saying, "Here, in the rapprochement subphase, we feel is the mainspring of man's eternal struggle against both fusion and isolation" (p.130). In Lichtenstein's (1963) terms, human existence is a matter of constant negotiation between "metamorphosis" or "identity." Dr. Kogan's paper misses this point.

CONCLUSION

By the way of presenting a clinical case in detail, Dr. Ilany Kogan has offered us major insights into craving for oneness. Her work is theoretically sophisticated and technically moving. However, in viewing the craving for oneness as mostly pathological, Dr. Kogan misses out on the rich tapestry of the human experience which invariably oscillates between safeguarding and losing its restricted boundaries. Symbiosis and separation pull at the self from opposite ends. Sometimes one extreme wins, sometimes the other. Sometimes life offers us opportunity to live out both extremes in an optimal synthesis. At other times, we have to wait till death. Note that Dr. Kogan's patient wanted to "sleep with his mother . . . in her grave." In that striving, he was hardly different from an old Hungarian woman in New York whose mother had perished in the Holocaust and who stipulated in her will that, after cremation, her ashes be sent back to Hungary and buried in her father's grave (Stepansky, 1988). By getting cremated, she identified with the mother who was sent to the ovens and by "sleeping" (forever) with her father, she defeated her oedipal mother. Themes of oneness and separateness were both posthumously realized by one grand gesture. The woman's name, incidentally, was Margaret Mahler!

REFERENCES

Akhtar, S. (1992a). *Broken Structures: Severe Personality Disorders and Their Treatment.* Northvale, NJ: Jason Aronson.
———. (1992b). Tethers, orbits, and invisible fences: Clinical, developmental, sociocultural, and technical aspects of optimal distance. In *When the Body Speaks: Psychological Meanings in Kinetic Clues,* eds. S. Kramer and S. Akhtar, pp. 21–57. Northvale, NJ: Jason Aronson.

———. (1995). *Quest for Answers: Understanding and Treating Severe Personality Disorders*. Northvale, NJ: Jason Aronson.

———. (1999). *Immigration and Identity: Turmoil, Treatment, and Transformation*. Northvale, NJ: Jason Aronson.

Anzieu, D. (1992). The sound image of the self. *International Review of Psychoanalysis* 6:23–32.

Benedek, T. (1938). Adaptation to reality in early infancy. *Psychoanalytic Quarterly* 7:200–214.

Bion, W. R. (1970). *Attention and Interpretation*. London: Tavistock Publications.

Chasseguet-Smirgel, J. (1984). *Creativity and Perversion*. New York: Norton.

Erikson, E. (1959). *Identity and the Life Cycle*. New York: International Universities Press.

Federn, P. (1952). *Ego Psychology and the Psychoses*. New York: Basic.

Freud, S. (1895). Project for a scientific psychology. *Standard Edition* 1:283–398.

———. (1900). Interpretation of dreams. *Standard Edition* 4:1–337.

———. (1911). Formulations on the two principles of mental functioning. *Standard Edition* 12:213–237.

———. (1913). On beginning the treatment. *Standard Edition* 12:121–144.

———. (1915). The unconscious. *Standard Edition* 14:159–237.

Gabbard, G., and Lester, E. (1995). *Boundaries and Boundary Violations in Psychoanalysis*. Washington, DC: American Psychiatric Press.

Gaddini, E. (1972). Aggression and the pleasure principle. *International Journal of Psychoanalysis* 53:191–197.

Grand, S. (2000). *The Reproduction of Evil: A Clinical and Cultural Perspective*. Hillsdale, NJ: The Analytic Press.

Hamilton, N. G. (1986). Positive projective identification. *International Journal of Psychoanalysis* 67:489–497.

Hartmann, H. (1969). *Ego and the Problem of Adaptation*. New York: International Universities Press.

Jacobson, E. (1964). *The Self and the Object World*. New York: International Universities Press.

Joseph, B. (1982). Addiction to near-death. In *Psychic Equilibrium and Psychic Change*, eds. M. Feldman and E. B. Spillius, pp. 127–139. London: Rutledge, 1991.

Killingmo, B. (1989). Conflict and deficit: Implications for technique. *International Journal of Psychoanalysis* 70:65–79.

Klein, M. (1946). Notes on some schizoid mechanism. In *Envy and Gratitude and Other Works 1946–1963*, pp. 1–24. New York: Free Press; rpt. 1975.

Klein, M. (1975). A contribution to the psychogenesis of manic-depressive states. In *Love, Guilt, and Reparation, and Other Works, 1921–1924*, pp. 262–289. New York: Free Press.

Kramer, S., and Akhtar, S. (1988). The developmental context of pre-oedipal internalized object relations. *Psychoanalytic Quarterly* 42:547–576.

Lichtenstein, H. (1963). The dilemma of human identity: Notes on self-transformation, self-objectivation, and metamorphosis. *Journal of the American Psychoanalytic Association* 11:173–223.

Loewald, H. (1960). On the therapeutic action of psychoanalysis. In *Papers on Psychoanalysis*. New Haven, CT: Yale University Press.

Mahler, M. S. (1972). A study of the separation and individuation process and its possible application to borderline phenomena in the psychoanalytic situation. *Psychoanalytic Study of the Child* 26:403–424.

Mahler, M. S., Pine, F., and Bergman, A. (1975). *The Psychological Birth of the Human Infant*. New York: Basic Books.

Neri, C. (2005). What is the function of faith and trust in psychoanalysis? *International Journal of Psychoanalysis* 86:79–97.

Pine, F. (1997). *Diversity and Direction in Psychoanalytic Technique*. New Haven, CT: Yale University Press.

Roland, A. (1988). *In Search of Self in India and Japan*. Princeton, NJ: Princeton University Press.

Sandler, J., and Sandler, A. M. (1983). The "second censorship," the "three-box model," and some technical implications. *International Journal of Psychoanalysis* 64:413–415.

Stepansky, P. E. (1988). *The Memoirs of Margaret S. Mahler*. New York: Free Press.

Winnicott, D. W. (1962). Ego integration in child developmental. In *The Maturational Processes and the Facilitating Environment*, pp. 56–64. New York: International Universities Press, 1975.

8

Why Boundaries, Fences, and Walls around the Self? A Concluding Commentary

Henri Parens, M.D.

Boundaries delineating and containing the self secure one's conscious and unconscious experience of entity and of self-governance. Self-boundaries are required as much by the self as the cell membrane is required by the cell contents (see Ruth Garfield's comparable use of this metaphor, this volume). Fences and walls on the other hand are erected in the face of threat to the self by forces outside the self, commonly, forces perceived as hostile or destructive, or both. In the process of developing self-boundaries, the developing organism surrounds itself by an optimal space that, determined by the nature of state, need, wishes, and here and now conditions, is highly accommodative and variable, from skin to skin contact or "null space," to condition-dependent distance. Reciprocally, this optimal space secures self-boundaries.

While biologically determined primary narcissism (I see Freud's assumption of primary narcissism as the psychological extension of the biological tendency of all living organisms to survive, both as individual and as member of the species) draws the limits of the emerging self, the child is not born with well-defined boundaries and consciously perceived optimal space. The degree to which boundaries become well defined and that optimal space (distance) evolves is a matter of experience and development; I assume that these form and reciprocally are formed by the qualitative development of the ego. In her chapter, Phyllis Tyson takes us through the multiple and complex dynamics of boundary formation.

BOUNDARIES AND THEIR FORMATION

In a well-informed effort to lay out the complexity of self and object bound-ary formation, Tyson views this formative process juxtaposing the linear phase-sequential process of separation-individuation and the systems model used by Bowlby to explicate attachment (1969, 1973). Louis Sander (1964, 1983) also used a systems model, though structured differently, to concep-tualize the development of the child within and by virtue of the nature of mother-child interactions.

Given that one's concept and experiencing of the boundaries of the other are totally self-dependent, it is by looking at the development of the self's boundaries that we understand the perceived boundaries of the other. De-tailing the process in question using the views of Bowlby, Mahler, and Win-nicott, Tyson reports on the models having engendered disagreements, "ten-sion" as she says. To try to demonstrate some of the "tension" to which Tyson refers between the loyalists of the two theories, I will use a set of diagrams: "Boundary formation." While the tension between the loyalists of both theo-ries is reduced, the tension between the models is nonetheless not resolved and the question is: can it, should it be resolved? A look at the figures that follow makes the problem clear.

Tyson observes that separation-individuation presents a plausible evolv-ing of boundary formation as the young child evolves from his psychically perceived self-object unity—through the separation-individuation process—to self and object as separate but bound by a powerful emotional bond. In this model boundary formation occurs from the differentiation subphase,

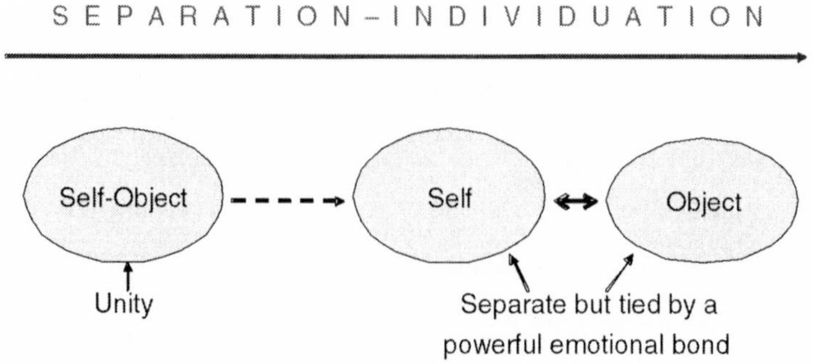

S E P A R A T I O N – I N D I V I D U A T I O N

Figure 8.1.   Boundary Formation in Separation-Individuation: From Self-Object Unity to Self and Object Relatedness

from hatching from the "symbiotic membrane" where self and object are perceived as predominantly coalesced even while observably evident—e.g., the 15-day-old infant, nursing, stares for minutes uninterruptedly into the mother's face—allowing the inference that self and other are intermittently perceived as separate even within the infant's "symbiotic self concept" (Parens, 1971). But "intermittently perceived" does not establish a boundary sufficiently since it does not assure the stability of the boundary. Once "hatched" during the differentiation subphase from the self-object containing symbiotic membrane, the infant now empowered by his narcissistic omnipotence and his obligatory "thrust to autonomy" (Parens, 1979; Parens et al., 1987), yielding the sense that "the world is his oyster" (Mahler, Pine, and Bergman, 1975), the self as agent as Tyson says, begins his explorations beyond the former symbiotic container membrane.

During this practicing subphase, his omnipotence not yet impeded by his soon to further differentiate cognitive abilities—the level which Piaget (1937) helped us to understand becomes possible by the middle of year two with the capacity for object permanence—even when feet away from his mother, the child behaves as if he does not yet fully recognize the separateness that in reality exists between self and mother. Can we assume that during this brief period of narcissistically fueled omnipotence the child is busy structuring a sound though very young, i.e., 11- to 18-month-old, sense of autonomy, that factor of such importance to the structuring of the self?

It is the maturation of cognition that helps thrust the child into the rapprochement subphase that the child recognizes the fact of his or her separateness at a newly perceived level of comprehension, a perception of reality that leads to a more or less intense rapprochement crisis as Mahler et al. (1975) described (see Parens, 1979, pp. 227–231 for a strikingly clear example of such a crisis). A space between self and object is now realistically perceived that will take the next 18 months or so to adapt to adequately. The as if all-at-once perceived reality creates an abysmal space to which the infant will react by taking on the task of defining, of establishing a self boundary of fundamental identity-organization, an increasingly stabilizing structure that Tyson defines as the self's "me as object" and "I" as self-agent. Elsewhere I described how a twin sitting next to her twin sister puzzlingly, tentatively, touched her own thigh, the one adjacent to her sister, then touched her sister's thigh, twice consecutively, allowing the inference that she was trying to determine whose thigh is whose, where she ends and her sister begins, identifying their separateness and the space between them (Parens et al., 1987).

With apology to the reader not as well versed in attachment theory, i.e., not knowing the attachment theory literature on boundary formation, it seems to me that we are led to assume that there is an inherent boundary awareness from the outset which then differentiates dramatically during the

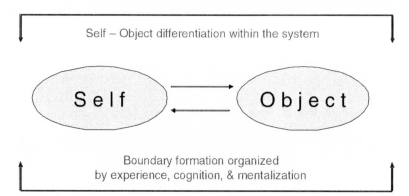

Figure 8.2. Boundary Formation: Within Self-Object System

ongoing attachment process. I would represent this development as in figure 8.2. Note that this model does not start from an assumed self-object unity, but rather from an assumed dyad, boundary formation then developing from within this already existing dyad.

Although this model does not specify a developmental line for boundary formation, nonetheless, I do not doubt that the model is amply adequate to explain how boundaries form within an already existing dyad. I press to say that a linear developmental model is not better than a systems model, nor is the systems model better than a linear model—a fallacy theory generators and their loyalists are at risk of entertaining. Rather, the complexity of human experience and function requires such multiconceptual models and explanations. The system models used by Bowlby and by Sander make us aware of specific qualitative dynamics in which boundary formation organizes. The linear model informs us of the sequential evolution of that interactional development. Here as in other aspects/sectors of psychic life, both systems and linear models enrich our understanding, demanding that we accept complexity in psychic development and life—as we so amply experience in our clinical work.

Now I want to look at the question of "tensions" created by and between these models. First, figure 8.3 illustrates that because the models do not start with the same assumption, i.e., what we postulate to be the child's psychological experiential state that best fits what we see in observing very young children, attempts to integrate them are impeded. In figure 8.3, juxtaposing or superimposing the models I try to conceptualize the problem.

How does the baby start? Lyons-Ruth (1991) rightly raises the question: At about 18 months, do we see a rapprochement or an approchement? The diagram suggests that if the baby starts in a self-object unity, then at 18 months

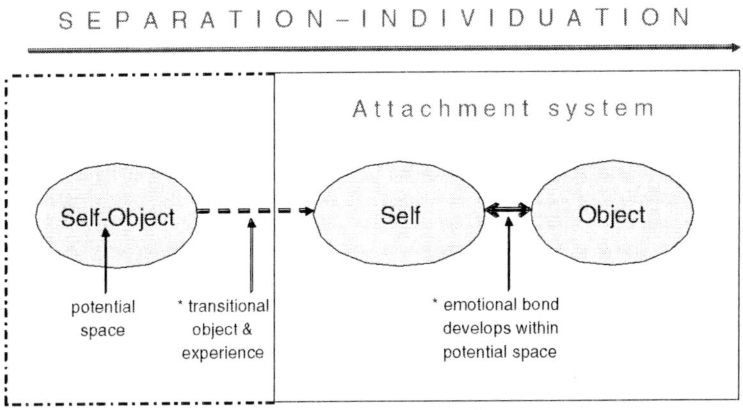

S E P A R A T I O N – I N D I V I D U A T I O N

Attachment system

Self-Object

Self

Object

potential
space

* transitional
object &
experience

* emotional bond
develops within
potential space

Figure 8.3.   Boundary Formation: From Self-Object Unity to Self and Object Relatedness?

there is a *ra*pprochement; once having been a unity with her, after his world-explorations, the infant returns to the surround near-mother. If the infant starts psychologically in a dyadic state, then Lyons-Ruth's question has much merit; the infant gives evidence of needing to be in the surround near-mother. Since the models give us a choice, we are at odds as to which of the two models most accurately represents the infant's likely state; but since we are seeking truth in a domain where inference rules, our best human efforts do not guarantee which is the true model. Agreement on this is not in sight.

Sander does not declare himself on this question. Winnicott says there is no baby there is only a "baby-mother." Stern holds that there is a perceived self from the outset which inclines him toward Bowlby's explanation except that despite his disclaimer about the merits of linear development, his model speaks of the emergence of the self in stages (Stern 1985). However, I do not believe these disagreements to be the principle source of the tension manifest around the greater merits of attachment theory versus ego psychology—which includes separation-individuation.

Tyson serves us well in demonstrating the richness of explanation yielded by skillfully using various models to explain specified sectors of experience. The tension produced by the differing models is easily offset by the gains Tyson illustrates. Rather, I question that ascribing tensions between separation-individuation theory and attachment theory resides in Bowlby's assertion that he developed a systems explanation for attachment because he could not "reduce" its complexity to a linear sequential-stages theory. While Lyons-Ruth plausibly raises question with Mahler's concept of rapprochement, the tension resulting from this questioning causes no injury to our theorizing; quite the contrary, our search for factual explanation is kept alive. Rather, tension originated from another well-established source.

The origins of the controversy surrounding attachment theory (i.e., Bowlby) versus mainstream ego psychology (i.e., versus Spitz and Mahler), I believe lie in the disastrous 1960 debacle between John Bowlby and Anna Freud so clearly evident in John Bowlby's 1958 pejorative misrepresentation of Anna Freud's drive theory explanation of early attachment, followed then by the blistering counterattacks on John Bowlby by Anna Freud, by Max Schur, and by Rene Spitz in the 1960 *Psychoanalytic Study of the Child.* The results of this interpersonal conflict heavily burdened the cogent disagreements that arise from the theoretic models. The toxic tension was not between the models but between the generators of the models. The models inform each other and enrich our understanding of this complex all-important process, the child's developing relatedness with his object world.

Rather than a discouraging tension between models I find it a dilemma to attempt to compare or test for truth among these two highly informative models. Just as Peter Wolff (1960) found when he attempted to integrate Piaget's epistemological development with psychoanalytic developmental theory, the obstacles to integration are insurmountable. We can only let each model inform us within the limits of its own conceptualization and it is up to us to use them in the service of our own enlightenment and facilitate our helping our patients. Just as Tyson juxtaposes attachment and separation-individuation to find explanation from each, so do I. Tyson also takes us to another crucial aspect of boundary formation.

Tyson cogently places the locus of boundary formation within the "potential space" of experience, one of Winnicott's unique contributions to understanding the young child's psychic life. She reminds us that the potential space is "an intermediate area of experiencing that [lays] between . . . the inner world . . . and actual or external reality." I find it problematic (that it also means) that it is the space that lies "between the subjective object and the object objectively perceived, between me-extensions and not-me" (p. 20). My grasp of these specifiers suggests that there are a number of potential spaces: one between inner experiencing and external reality; another, the transitional space, the internally perceived interactional space between self and external object that yields the transitional object in the face of separation anxiety; then the space "between the subjective object [is this the 'self-object'"of Kohut?] and the objectively perceived object, or the me-extensions and not-me." Boundary of self and therewith of the object would be formed between the subjectively experienced self as contained on the inner side of that potential space, while simultaneously placing the object (other) on the outer side of that space—that self-protecting space that eventually organizes into "optimal distance." I want to add one more comment in contribution to Tyson's effort.

Regarding the role of the "libido/hostile destructiveness gradient" (Parens, 2005) in boundary formation, Tyson tells us that "Complexity and challenge begin to characterize interactions as the toddler begins to experience limits and expectations—I have found these to begin even from 6 months of age on" (Parens, 1979; Parens et al., 1987). One of the largest problems that befall parents is limit-setting, that unavoidable, protective, and civilizing function the child exacts from his parents. While limit-setting is one of the experiences that most predictably creates an interpersonal conflict between child and parent that brings with it an acute state of interpersonal hostility (if not rage)—the foremost reason most parents and children wish these did not happen—this troubling challenge brings with it much benefit for the child, e.g., civilizing and protecting the child against harm. But an additional benefit is that perhaps more than a secure love attachment, hostile destructiveness generated in the child by the parent's limit-setting sharply delineates the child's sense of self and of object. Of course, so do other experiential generators of hostile destructiveness in the child.

The conflict created in us when we hate the person we love, ambivalence, is all too well known. The ego draws a line between the polarizing affects (Mahler, 1968; Kernberg, 1982, 1992), much as Anna Freud told us that the line between the ego and the superego is discernible dynamically most commonly in the face of an interagency conflict—in accord with the structural model. The polarity of love feelings and hostile/hate feelings, constituting an intrapsychic conflict, pushes to delineate self from the pain-inducing-hate-generating object. I suggest (2003 [2005]) then that this coexistence of love and hate constitutes a gradient of love/hate (libido/hostile destructiveness) that contributes importantly to the delimitation of self and the pain-inducing other. Obviously, the degree of hostility generated in the child by the parent's action, if too intense, while delineating self from object, will bring with it intense affects that can create much difficulty on their own. Just as a tolerable degree of anxiety in the face of not knowing how to solve an algebraic problem compels the child to learn to do so and too much anxiety interferes with the child's learning to do so, so too, degrees of hostility generated in the child may induce growth or interfere with growth, developmental, cognitive, and psychic.

Parenthetically, I do not believe as Tyson seems to suggest that the child's perception of the object as hurtful and hateful results from the child's projections of his own hostility. Rather, when the object intentionally hurts—unavoidably so perceived when the parent sets limits—the young child perceives the object as factually hurtful, which generates hostility in the child and eventually hate; this perception does not result from projection, although the projection of the child's own hostility will add to the hostility experienced toward the parent.

But our boundaries are often challenged; at times the challenge is in our best interest; sometimes it is not. Whether in our best interest or not, the challenge to our boundaries pushes us to secure our borders; we may erect fences and even walls.

FENCES AND WALLS

Just as we do in external reality, we set up fences and walls around ourselves to mark the boundaries of what is one's own, be it oneself or one's possessions, to selectively choose those who enter our sphere of experience and activity. Of course, walls secure our safety and seal us off more than do fences. In our psychic life, fences and walls are erected to secure the integrity of our sense of self and to draw the line of our sense of optimal distance. Securing one's safety by means of walls, as we know from clinical work, may maintain fragile self-integrity but can be costly when access to selective others is denied. Both Gabbard and Kogan take us there. Gabbard lucidly speaks to the analyst breaching the patient's self-containing boundaries. Kogan takes us into the domain of the patient breaching, quite dramatically, the analyst's self boundaries-as-analyst.

Gabbard, one of the best minds on boundary violations in the clinical situation (Gabbard and Lester, 1995), tells us that the domain of boundary violation is wide, so much so, he holds, that at one end of the spectrum are behaviors we consider outright violations that cause much harm, and at the other end are boundary-challenging behaviors that do not constitute violations but rather a benign, even beneficial challenge to them. Pointing out "the widening scope of analysis" (Stone, 1954) warranted for more traumatized and troubled patients who require some modification of technique beyond interpretation has created an area of boundary vagueness challenging to the clinician. We understand today better than before that in order for the analyst to engage in an analytic process, the analyst must with integrity and with care permit himself to subjectively experience his interactions with the patient. This however, as Gabbard referring to Mitchell (1993) notes, must be done "in a way that the patient can find enriching rather than demolishing" (p. 40). The process of analysis itself requires a subjective engagement on the part of the analyst in order to make himself emotionally accessible to the patient as "a transference object or series of objects." While objectivity is highly desirable in all scientific and therapeutic endeavors, it is required but insufficient to create an analytic process. But, though we no longer doubt that subjectivity is required of the analyst to make an analytic process possible, we know equally well that this facilitates the analyst's countertransference reactivity.

This, Gabbard believes, makes it that "countertransference enactments are inevitable and . . . create minor versions of boundary transgressions throughout the treatment" (p. 40). But these, having a benign and even beneficial effect on the patient, must be differentiated from violations. The former, Gabbard has proposed, are "boundary crossings" (Gutheil and Gabbard, 1993, 1998). Acknowledging the complexity and at times vagueness of boundary violation versus boundary crossing, Gabbard makes the difference between them quite clear: Does the analyst's action clinically benefit the patient, is of itself therapeutic for the patient, for whom interpretation does not lead to a perceptible working through process, the essential labor that makes analysis work? Does the analyst's action clinically harm, even injure the patient, a fact to which the analyst is blinded by virtue of his resistance to perceiving his own countertransference? Even where the line between the two may not be painted in neon colors, the analyst's integrity and his ability to ascertain his own countertransference are paramount to his knowing where the line lies.

As do boundary violations, boundary crossings vary widely too. Not long ago, in conversation with an estimable gentleman at a luncheon, he revealed to me that he had been in analysis for many, many years. He feels he truly benefited from it. But, he said tentatively, his analyst seemed to at times tell him about some of his own personal concerns; the man thought, maybe because he was older than his doctor. And the man said, "You know, I didn't like that. It made me feel very uncomfortable." In contrast to several other cases where much harm was caused by the analyst, in this case, the analyst's occasionally sharing his concerns with his older patient caused the patient some discomfort and he wished his analyst had not done that. Clearly, this instance of self-disclosure, while certainly of no value to the patient and reflective of a lack of technical discipline on the part of the analyst did not cause harm; in fact, seeing my response of modest critical disapproval, my interlocutor seemed to chuckle about it. Perhaps he had made me the target of his benign criticism of his analyst.

I have lived the question of being a self-disclosing analyst in a much more serious context. I measure it as a significant boundary crossing, though not vis-à-vis one particular patient. As a psychoanalyst long in practice, but also as a Holocaust survivor, I have had to face the dilemma of "bearing witness to the Holocaust" and maintaining as best as I have been able to the degree of anonymity psychoanalysis warrants—a real challenge to a faculty member of a training institute. I have long tried to maintain whatever anonymity is possible in a training center—even though I was once encouraged, indeed directed, by our Psychoanalytic Institute director to go public with our prevention efforts that would expose me in action outside of the analytic situation, i.e., parenting education (Parens et al., 1979). But now in the eighth decade of my life, the challenge to my maintaining an optimal degree of anonymity was different: I could no longer wait; I had to bear witness. That meant I had to write my "witness report" and had to be willing to speak out about it. Painfully, I wrote my Holocaust memoirs (Parens, 2004). By the way, in the book I address the question of why it has taken survivors so long to tell of their own specific experiences, and had to add why for myself as a psychoanalyst I waited so many years to do so.

In a section entitled "The Doctor as Burden to His Patients" (pp. 178–181), I attempt to explain to a lay reader why and how my self-disclosure might create a more or less significant burden for my patients: "Patients come to us because they have hurtful and handicapping problems of their own with which they want us to help them; they do not need in addition to take on their analyst's life burdens" (p. 179). And I have heard directly at least some of the consequences of my having written those memoirs; I have opened myself to questions and reactions by my patients and am dealing with the matter as a reality-based issue, keeping an eye on the implications of my book and our discussions of it on the treatment of the patient. I have also made myself available for talking about this to former patients. From the evidence I have, I trust that this is a boundary crossing which, while it has caused them some pain, has not harmed my patients. I should note that my self disclosure did not impose itself on my patients from within the clinical setting. But of course, unavoidably, even though I disclosed it outside the domain of transference-countertransference, its reverberations have reached there.

BOUNDARY VIOLATIONS BY PATIENTS

In a richly clinically and conceptually detailed chapter, Ilany Kogan presents us with a troubling but quite less often considered matter, the complement to the analyst's boundary crossings and violations; she reports on one of her patient's bewildering challenge to her self-boundary as psychoanalyst. As an aside, while we often speak of patients' acting out, we do not often consider these behaviors in terms of boundary violation. The title of Kogan's chapter, "Breaking of Boundaries and Craving for Oneness" conveys the thrust of the patient's actions: in his transference-bound craving for oneness, he broke boundaries, "analytical boundaries of time, place, and abstinence of touch," seemingly driven to insinuate himself into a "symbiosis with her."

While this patient presented many clinical challenges, among the most troubling to Kogan was the patient's breaching the boundaries of her self-as-analyst, intruding into her personal-self life at a time quite painful for her. As Kogan tells us, while she was mourning the loss of her own beloved father, her patient breached the privacy of her *shiva* (mourning wake), omnipotently and sadistically forcing himself into the privacy of her mourning. During this very troubling intrusion, to make matters further intrusive, the patient, who had lost his 20-year-old son in a suicide, witnessed Kogan's own son come onto the scene and greet her affectionately.

Serious trauma compelled this egregious boundary violation on the part of her patient. Reared by parents who were seriously traumatically mentally disordered by their Holocaust experiences—and were no doubt burdened by psychological problems that preceded the Holocaust (Parens, 1999)—the patient's separation-individuation was seriously derailed by interaction with his very sick mother and feebly present father, eventuating in the patient's having a near-fulfilled incestuous relationship with his mother who subsequently died in a suicide, leaving him in a very difficult to resolve state of mourning. As Kogan suggests, this then led to his being driven to reenact his unresolved symbiotic yearnings with her, his analyst. Mourning, which would require a separation from the object of the symbiosis, was interfered with, leaving him with no end of interpersonal difficulties, including the loss of his own son by suicide at age 20 and no end of self-object boundary violations. Kogan tells us, "The reality of the trauma intruded . . . by breaking boundaries between fantasy and reality, and hampering both the patient's and the analyst's ability to symbolize." The challenge to the analyst's ability to function analytically, one familiar to many of us in the face of such patient acting out, is large.

While this chapter deserves extensive discussion on a number of points, I select one aspect of the difficulties Kogan encountered for further thought. Kogan rightly feels that her ability to help the patient mourn, therewith engendering boundary formation heretofore unachieved, was a cardinal achievement of the analysis. But to achieve that end, she had to labor in the mines of her own experience of this patient: "Although my patient was at times depressed and helpless, [I experienced] him as a powerful menacing figure who could destroy me and the treatment. . . . [And she wondered if she] could continue analytic work with this violent, frightening patient." Astute clinically, when she worked through her own reactive shock and amazement at the patient's brazen boundary violation, she "became aware of the patient's own fear of his uncontrollable aggression."

I would emphasize Kogan's maintaining governance over the countertransference hostility his varied boundary violations generated in her—in addition to that unavoidably activated in her by his sadistic transference—and her ability to maintain her analytic stance and analyze the patient's conviction that driven by his long accumulated murderous wishes he caused not only the death of his mother but of his own son as well. Analyzing and working through her own rage at her patient, she could withstand his attacks on her and the treatment. She therewith demonstrated to the patient that his own omnipotent dangerousness was not as dangerous as he in his youthful fantasies had imagined and feared. One might engender in the patient the realization that "My dangerousness, heretofore affirmed by the suicides of my mother and my son both of which I caused, may not be real since, as I see, I am not destroying you." Gabbard (1991) reported much the same experience with a man whose rage he withstood, a rage that challenged and threatened the therapy, much to the patient's surprise and eventual gratitude.

The challenges the patient put to Kogan included her recognizing that she had been threatened by him, perceiving the patient as a monstrous father who might well have induced his own son's suicide. Kogan's associations were to the legends of Chronos and Saturn, fathers who devoured their own children. Her associations, I felt, revealed a possible contributory source to her feeling threatened by this patient. Did our skilled and admirable colleague—whose own son came onto the boundary violation *shiva* scene and greeted his mother affectionately—forget to also list Medea along with Chronos and Saturn? Might not such a patient disturb any of us so sharply, at least in part, because he makes us perceive resonances within ourselves of even if only rarely experienced wishes to destroy our own beloved children? Patients as these frighten us both from within their transferences to us and from within our own repressed, totally unacceptable however transient filicidal wishes. I forgive Kogan, I would any of us, for having left out of her associations that Medea too devoured her children (by proxy, feeding them to Jason, their father). Yes, we sane, loving, responsible humans can have such wishes—I repeat, however briefly experienced—heavily outweighed and inhibited/neutralized by our own voluminous love for our children. The dynamics of our own love/hate gradient play their part.

These very challenging but not factually dangerous patients, who do not threaten physical crime, are so challenging because they stir in us our innermost vulnerabilities—be it our once upon a time deeply dreaded fear of abandonment, or our barbaric murderous wishes and fantasies toward those we love deeply. Here is my preaching lesson for the day: He/she who is in touch with these deeply set vulnerabilities will not fear his/her not factually dangerous patients.

Just one more thought. Kogan tells us: "Recovering my ability to symbolize and relate to his murderous wishes as an infantile fantasy and not a reality created a new analytic space in which the patient was no longer a threat to me, and in which we could work through the mourning of his son as well as his mother" (p. 82). "Analytic space?" is my question, the space created for analyzing. We use that, as Tyson did, the "play space" where the child analyst works. I think that such a "positive being together space" is created by what the Lou Sander and Dan Stern Boston study group have identified as "now moments" (Stern, 2001, 2004), a jointly experienced epiphany, an intersubjective event in which the relationship of the patient and analyst is modified positively and facilitates the analytic work. The "analytic space" made possible by such "now moments" in turn made it possible for Kogan to do the exemplary analytic work she did, to progressively help the patient establish self and object boundaries engendering the patient's ability to mourn.

CONCLUSION

Psychic boundaries establish with the structuring of self, are made possible by the collaboration of objects in one's emotional environment, and in turn structure the boundaries of the objects. Like the development of basic trust or basic mistrust, where the object is trusted, so is the self (Erikson, 1959); self boundaries are established in parallel with our establishing the boundaries of the perceived object. Where the object in the environment encroaches or threatens to encroach on the optimal distance we establish around ourselves defensive fences and where needed, even walls are erected to protect the vulnerable integrity of the self.

REFERENCES

Bowlby, J. A. (1958). The nature of the child's tie to his mother. *International Journal of Psycho-Analysis* 39:350–373.

———. (1960). Grief and mourning in infancy and early childhood. *Psychoanalytic Study of the Child* 15:9–52.

———. (1969). *Attachment*. New York: Basic.

———. (1973). *Attachment and Loss, Vol. 2: Separation*. New York: Basic.

Erikson, E. H. (1959). *Identity and the Life Cycle*. New York: International Universities Press.

Freud, A. (1960). Discussion of Dr. John Bowlby's paper. *Psychoanalytic Study of the Child* 15:53–62.

Gabbard, G. O. (1991). Technical approaches to the transference hate in the analysis of borderline patients. *International Journal of Psycho-Analysis* 72:625–638.

———. (2005). Sexual and nonsexual boundary violations in psychoanalysis and psychotherapy. Presented at the 36th Annual Margaret Mahler Symposium, May 7, 2005, Philadelphia.

———, and Lester, E. P. (1995). *Boundary Violations in Psychoanalysis*. New York: Basic.

Gutheil, T. G., and Gabbard, G. O. (1993). The concept of boundaries in clinical practice: Theoretical enriched management dimensions. *American Journal of Psychiatry* 150:188–196.

———. (1998). Misuses and misunderstandings in boundary theory in clinical and regulatory settings. *American Journal of Psychiatry* 155:409–414.

Kernberg, O. F. (1982). Self, ego, affects and drives. *Journal of the American Psychoanalytic Association* 30:893–917.

———. (1992). *Aggression in Personality Disorders and Perversions*. New Haven, CT: Yale University Press.

Kogan, I. (2005). "Breaking boundaries and craving for oneness." Presented at the 36th Annual Margaret Mahler Symposium, May 7, 2005, Philadelphia.

Lyons-Ruth, K. (1991). Rapprochement or approchement: Mahler's theory reconsidered from the vantage point of recent research on early attachment relationships. *Psychoanalytic Psychology* 8:1–23.

Mahler, M. S. (1968). *On Human Symbiosis and the Vicissitudes of Individuation* (with M. Furer). New York: International Universities Press.

———, Pine, F., and Bergman, A. (1975). *Psychological Birth of the Human Infant*. New York: Basic.

Mitchell, S. A. (1993). *Hope and Dread in Psychoanalysis*. New York: Basic Books.

Parens, H. (1971). A contribution of separation-individuation to the development of psychic structure. In *Separation-Individuation: Essays in Honor of Margaret S. Mahler*, eds. J. B. McDevitt and C. F. Settlage, pp. 100–112. New York: International Universities Press.

———. (1979). *The Development of Aggression in Early Childhood*. New York: Jason Aronson, Inc.

———. (1999). Some influences of the Holocaust on development—one man's experience. Plenary addressed to the Annual Meeting of the American College of Psychoanalysts, May 15, 1999, Washington, DC. (Unpublished.)

———. (2004). *Renewal of Life—Healing from the Holocaust*. Rockville, MD: Schreiber Publishing.

———. (2005). Les vicissitudes de l'agression dans le processus deséparation-individuation et dans l'attachement. *Devenir* 17:183–209.

———, Scattergood, E., Hernit, R. C., and Duff, S. (1979). *Parenting: Love and Much More*. A Series of 39 Half-Hour Programs for Television. Taped for Broadcasting by CBS-WCAU Channel 10, Philadelphia, PA. June–July 1979.

Parens, H., Scattergood, E., Singletary, W., and Duff, A. (1987). *Aggression in Our Children: Coping with it Constructively*. Northvale, NJ: Jason Aronson, Inc.

———. (1997). *Parenting for Emotional Growth: A Curriculum for Students in Grades K Thru 12. Vol. 1, The Textbook; Vol. 2, The Lesson Plans*. Philadelphia: Parenting for Emotional Growth.

Piaget, J. (1937). *The Construction of Reality in the Child*. New York: Basic, 1954.

Sander, L. (1964). Adaptive relationships in early mother-child interaction. *Journal of the American Academy of Child Adolescent Psychiatry* 3:231–264.

———. (1983). Polarity, paradox and the organizing process in development. In *Frontiers of Infant Psychiatry, Vol. 2*, eds. J. D. Call, E. Galenson, and R. I. Tyson, pp. 333–346. New York: Basic.

Schur, M. (1960). Discussion of Dr. John Bowlby's paper. *Psychoanalytic Study of the Child* 15:63–84.

Spitz, R. (1960). Discussion of Dr. John Bowlby's paper. *Psychoanalytic Study of the Child* 15:85–94.

Stern, D. (1985). *The Interpersonal World of the Human Infant*. New York: Basic.

———. (2001). Research presented at The Psychoanalysis of Change and Change in Psychoanalysis Symposium in honor of Dr. Lotte Koehler, Munich, January 21, 2001. Muenchner Forum fuer neuere Entwicklungen in Psychoanalyse e. V.

———. (2004). *The Present Moment in Psychotherapy and Everyday Life*. New York: Norton.

Stone, L. (1954). The widening scope of indications for psychoanalysis. *Journal of the American Psychoanalytic Association* 2:567–594.

Tyson, P. (2005). Boundary formation in children: Normality and pathology. Presented at the 36th Annual Margaret Mahler Symposium, May 7, 2005, Philadelphia.

Wolff, P. H. (1960). *The Developmental Psychologies of Jean Piaget and Psychoanalysis*. New York: International Universities Press.

Index

About the Editor and Contributors

Salman Akhtar, M.D., is professor of psychiatry, Jefferson Medical College; training and supervising analyst, Psychoanalytic Center of Philadelphia, Philadelphia, PA.

Jennifer Bonovitz, Ph.D., is training and supervising analyst, Psychoanalytic Center of Philadelphia; cochair, South-Asia Forum of the Psychoanalytic Center of Philadelphia, Philadelphia, PA.

Ira Brenner, M.D., is clinical professor of psychiatry, Jefferson Medical College; training and supervising analyst, Psychoanalytic Center of Philadelphia, Philadelphia, PA.

Glen Gabbard, M.D., is joint editor-in-chief, *International Journal of Psychoanalysis*; Brown Foundation, chair of psychoanalysis and professor of psychiatry, Baylor College of Medicine, Houston, TX.

Ruth Garfield, M.D., is codirector, Child Psychotherapy Program, Psychoanalytic Center of Philadelphia, Philadelphia, PA.

Ilany Kogan, M.A., is member of the Advisory Board of the Fritz Bauer Holocaust Research Institute, Frankfurt, Germany; member of the Steering Committee of the Trauma Network, Hamburg, Germany; training analyst, Israel Psychoanalytic Society, Rehovot, Israel.

Henri Parens, M.D., is professor of psychiatry, Jefferson Medical College; training and supervising analyst, Psychoanalytic Center of Philadelphia, Philadelphia, PA.

Phyllis Tyson, Ph.D., is clinical professor of psychiatry, University of California at San Diego; training and supervising analyst, and child supervisor, San Diego Psychoanalytic Institute, San Diego, CA.